Inch'on 1950

The last great amphibious assault

Campaign • 162

Inch'on 1950

The last great amphibious assault

Gordon L Rottman • Illustrated by Peter Dennis

First published in Great Britain in 2006 by Osprey Publishing, Midland House, West Way, Botley, Oxford OX2 0PH, United Kingdom.
E-mail: info@ospreypublishing.com

ISBN 1 84176 961 4

Design: The Black Spot
Index by Alan Thatcher
Maps by The Map Studio
3D bird's eye views by John Plumer
Battlescene artwork by Graham Turner
Originated by The Electronic Page Company, Cwmbran, UK
Printed in China through World Print Ltd.

06 07 08 09 10   10 9 8 7 6 5 4 3 2 1

For a catalog of all books published by Osprey please contact:

NORTH AMERICA
Osprey Direct, C/o Random House Distribution Center, 400 Hahn Road, Westminster, MD 21157, USA
E-mail: info@ospreydirect.com

ALL OTHER REGIONS
Osprey Direct UK, P.O. Box 140, Wellingborough, Northants, NN8 2FA, UK
E-mail: info@ospreydirect.co.uk

www.ospreypublishing.com

Acknowledgments

The author wishes to thank Don Boose (Col, USA, Ret) and the staff of the US Marine Corps Historical Center.

Abbreviations

AAA	anti-aircraft artillery
AbnDiv	Airborne Division
Amtrac	amphibian tractor (see LVT)
APD	High-speed transport (aka destroyer-transport)
ARCT	Airborne Regimental Combat Team
BCT	Battalion Combat Team
CavDiv	Cavalry Division
DD	Destroyer
FBHL	Force Beachhead Line
FECOM	Far East Command
InfDiv	Infantry Division
JCS	Joint Chiefs of Staff (US)
JTF7	Joint Task Force Seven
KATUSA	Korean Augmentation to the US Army
KMC	Korean Marine Corps
KPA	Korean People's Army (NK)
LCM	Landing Craft, Mechanized
LCVP	Landing Craft, Vehicle and Personnel
LSM(R)	Landing Ship, Medium (Rocket)
LST	Landing Ship, Tank
LSU	Landing Ship, Utility
LVT(A)5	Landing Vehicle, Tracked (Armored) Mk V
LVT(3)C	Landing Vehicle, Tracked Mk III Covered (amtrac)
MarDiv	Marine Division
NK	North Korea (Democratic People's Republic of Korea), North Koreans
Prov MarBde	Provisional Marine Brigade
RCT	Regimental Combat Team
ROK	Republic of Korea (South Korea)
ROKA	Republic of Korea Army
TF	Task Force
UN	United Nations
US	United States
USMC	United States Marine Corps
(-)	less (elements detached from parent unit)
(+)	reinforced (additional elements attached)

Battalions organic to US Marine and Army regiments are designated with the battalion and regimental number, for example: 1/5 Marines=1st Battalion, 5th Marines; 2/32 Infantry=2d Battalion, 32d Infantry Regiment. Companies and batteries are designated, for example B/10=Battery B, 1st Battalion, 10th Marines and the battalion designation not shown.

US Marine and Army Officer Ranks

2dLt	2nd Lieutenant
1stLt	1st Lieutenant
Capt	Captain
Maj	Major
LtCol	Lieutenant Colonel
Col	Colonel
BGen	Brigadier General ("one-star")
MajGen	Major General ("two-star")
LtGen	Lieutenant General ("three-star")
Gen	General ("four-star")

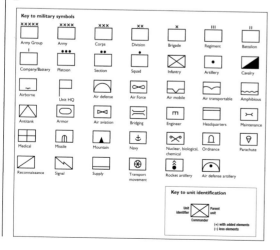

CONTENTS

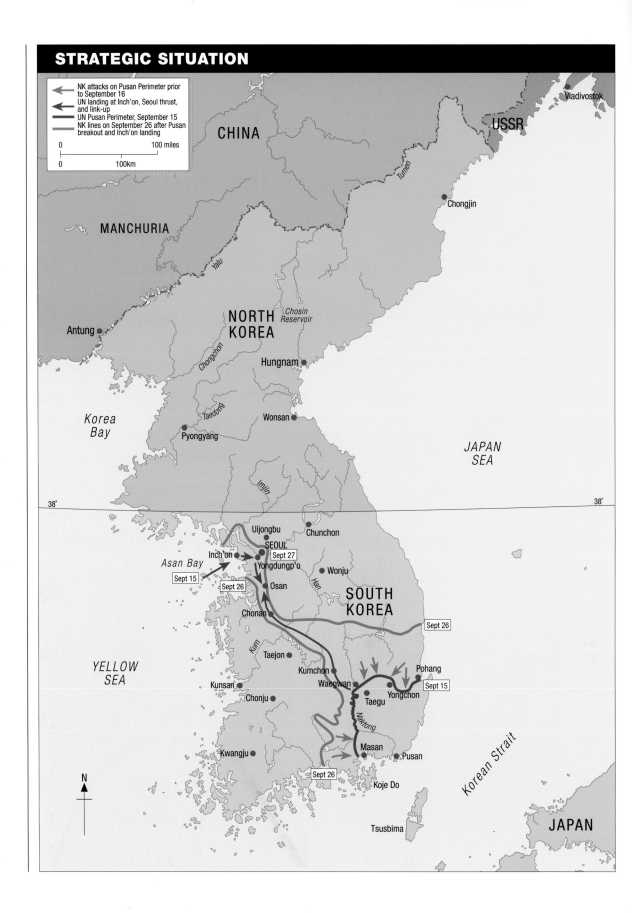

STRATEGIC SITUATION

NK attacks on Pusan Perimeter prior to September 16
UN landing at Inch'on, Seoul thrust, and link-up
UN Pusan Perimeter, September 15
NK lines on September 26 after Pusan breakout and Inch'on landing

0   100 miles
0   100km

CHINA

USSR

Vladivostok

MANCHURIA

Chongjin

Yalu

NORTH KOREA

Chosin Reservoir

Antung

Chongchon

Hungnam

Korea Bay

Taedong

Wonsan

JAPAN SEA

Pyongyang

Imjin

38°

38°

Uijongbu

Chunchon

SEOUL

Inch'on

Sept 27

Asan Bay

Yongdungp'o

Wonju

Sept 15

Sept 26

Osan

Han

SOUTH KOREA

Chonan

YELLOW SEA

Kum

Taejon

Kumchon

Pohang

Kunsan

Waegwan

Sept 26

Chonju

Yongchon

Sept 15

Taegu

Naktong

Kwangju

Masan

Pusan

Sept 26

Koje Do

N

Tsusbima

JAPAN

Korean Strait

ORIGINS OF THE CAMPAIGN

Korea (*Chosan* in Korean, *Chosen* to the Japanese) had been an empire since 2333 BC. Its strategic location meant that it was coveted by both China and Japan, empires with which Korea experienced varied and complex relations, never as allies, but as a country desired as something to possess. Japan occupied Korea during the 1904–05 Japan–Russian War and annexed it in 1910. They undertook extensive efforts to incorporate Korea into the empire in order to exploit its resources and people. Koreans were third-class citizens within their own land, and the Japanese ran all aspects of the colony, from the government to installing Japanese managers to operate businesses. Japanese was taught in schools, and all facets of Korean culture and traditions were suppressed. It even became mandatory for Koreans to adopt Japanese names. During World War II the Japanese exploited Korean industry and agriculture to support their war effort. Millions of Koreans were drafted into the armed forces, employed in industry, or even shipped to Japan, and forced into service as laborers and comfort women throughout the occupied countries.

With the end of the war, XXIV US Corps occupied southern Korea on September 4, 1945 while the Soviet Red Army occupied the north from August 12, the dividing line being the 38th Parallel just north of Seoul. While the United Nations sought national elections to re-unify the country, it was not to be. Backed by the USSR and Communist

South Korean refugees wait their turn to cross the Han River as the North Koreans approach. The military would not let them cross on the bridges for fear of saboteurs, so log and plank rafts were built alongside the supports. The bridges were destroyed on June 28. (USMC)

China, the Democratic People's Republic of Korea – North Korea (NK) – was established on August 15, 1948 with no intention of uniting with the south unless it was in control. Soviet occupation forces departed in December 1948 leaving their equipment behind. The division was unequal in both area and population. The south consisted of 37,000 square miles and a population of 21 million, while the north had 9 million people in 48,000 square miles.

The Korean People's Army (KPA) was formally established on August 15, 1948, but its formation had begun in 1946 under cover of the Peace Preservation Corps. Combat units were covertly organized under the guise of security force training schools, which provided leaders and cadres for the first divisions. By the time of the North Korean invasion of the south, three corps, ten infantry divisions, an armored brigade, and numerous support and security units had been raised, along with a small air force and navy, as well as a border constabulary. The USSR provided thousands of advisers, and most of the weapons, equipment, munitions, and supplies to the KPA, in addition to training thousands of technicians and specialists inside the USSR. At the time of the invasion the KPA contained 223,080 troops.

The Republic of Korea (ROK – pronounced "rock"), was proclaimed on August 15, 1948 after UN-supervised elections.[1] The ROK Army (ROKA) was established on the same date from the existing Korean Constabulary, which itself dated from 1946. The last US occupation troops departed in June 1949. At the time of the invasion the fledgling ROKA possessed eight under-strength and partly trained and equipped divisions with a total of 98,000 men. Besides securing the 38th Parallel, part of the army was engaged in combating northern guerrillas.

The Communist invasion caught the US and ROK completely by surprise when NK troops poured across the 38th Parallel at 0400hrs on June 25, 1950. The main North Korean attack was aimed at Seoul, and the

[1] The UN recognized the ROK on December 15, but it was not admitted to the UN until 1991, as was North Korea.

victorious divisions continued to press south. Events occurred rapidly. US forces were authorized to conduct combat operations; the UN passed a resolution approving the use of armed force to restore peace; Seoul fell three days after the invasion and Inch'on on July 3. A small US combat element, Task Force Smith, was deployed to Korea from Japan arriving on July 1 and was defeated two days later. Subsequent US efforts were defeated and the battered ROKA was pushed south. US units, inadequately trained and equipped from occupation duty in Japan, were rushed in, along with Commonwealth forces. Efforts to establish defensive lines failed and the UN forces were pushed into the southeast corner by August 4 to make what many perceived as a last stand at Pusan. UN reinforcements continued to arrive and for the next month and a half the NK forces battered themselves against a stout defense. By mid-September the NK divisions were spent and few reinforcements arrived. Their ammunition and supplies were running out, while the UN forces within the perimeter continued to receive reinforcements and supplies.

Even before the tide had turned against the North Koreans, Gen Douglas MacArthur was making plans to break out of the Pusan perimeter, conduct a dramatic outflanking amphibious assault to cut the enemy's supply line, and drive them north beyond the 38th Parallel. For an army tottering on the brink of defeat just weeks before, the plan could be considered nothing but bold and audacious, and, many said, bound to fail.

Reduced forces

In mid-1950 the US Army and Marine Corps were a shadow of themselves five years previously, as were the navy and the air force (which had only become service separate from the army in 1947). The US armed forces had just undergone a major transformation. Instead of separate departments of war and navy co-ordinated by the Joint Chiefs of Staff (JCS), they were now under the Department of Defense, of which the JCS was a component. Answering to the Department of Defense were the departments of the army, navy, and air force. A civilian secretary headed each department, who answered to the the president, the Commander-in-Chief.

While all the armed services suffered from rapid postwar reductions, the Army was in particularly bad shape. It had declined in size from 89 divisions on V-J Day, to seven infantry, two airborne, and one armored division in 1950. With the exception of the 1st InfDiv in Germany and the 82d Airborne Division (AbnDiv) in the States, all were severely under strength. Rather than the 18,804 men they should have mustered at full strength, they contained between 11,000 and 13,650 men. The Army itself was authorized 610,900 personnel, but only 593,000 were on the rolls. The divisions were essentially gutted. The three infantry regiments lacked their third battalions; each battalion had only two companies, and the companies themselves only two platoons. There were 36 rifle platoons in a division instead of the required 81. Divisional tank and AAA battalions had only a single company/battery and lacked a battalion headquarters. Field artillery and engineer battalions had only two companies/batteries. The batteries had four howitzers instead of six. Infantry regiment tank companies were non-existent. Other divisional units were likewise reduced and older equipment was mostly in use for training, which also suffered. Emphasis was placed on providing training in skills useful in the civilian world as well as civilian education. Combat training was seldom undertaken and then only at the small unit level. The four infantry divisions (1st Cavalry, 7th, 24th, 25th Infantry) on occupation duty in Japan were in even worse shape because of training restrictions. The poor state of Japanese roads and bridges meant that only light tanks were issued. Live range-firing was almost unheard of. The turnover rate was over 40 percent a year.

The Marine Corps was in equally dire straits – if not worse. The corps consisted of two under-strength divisions, down from six wartime units. Few support units existed and Marine Aviation consisted of 16 squadrons, four with jets. Of the 74,279 marines, fewer than one third were in the Fleet Marine Force, the corps' combat units. The 1st Marine Division (MarDiv) in California had 8,000 men with only one three-battalion regiment and a single artillery battalion. The 2d MarDiv in North Carolina had two infantry regiments, but one had only two battalions, and three artillery battalions to total 9,000 troops. War-strength divisions were authorized at 22,000 troops. It was intended that combat units would be removed from the Marine Corps, and their ground and air assets would be redeployed to the other services, reducing the service to a naval base security force and provider of troops to ships' detachments.

To aggravate this situation, even though the US was now expected to be deployable worldwide because of the emerging Cold War conflicts, only limited sea and airlift deployment capabilities existed. Overseas logistics infrastructure was also wanting. The US was ill-prepared to deploy and sustain combat forces in remote underdeveloped theaters. The US armed forces, though, had one thing going for them: many of the officers (even at company level) and the NCOs had combat experience. Command and control systems, logistics support, training techniques, and tactics were well developed, and the many lessons learned during World War II had been studied and incorporated into doctrine.

The 11th Marines' 105mm M2A1 howitzer prepares for a fire mission. Three battalions in both marine and Army divisions were armed with this excellent weapon. (USMC)

The Eighth US Army occupying Japan was mainly concerned with defending the Home Islands in the event of invasion by the USSR – an unlikely scenario. No planning was conducted for contingency operations in the Far East in response to small-scale regional conflicts. No defensive plans were made for Korea.

When the NK hordes swarmed across the 38th Parallel, the four occupation divisions in Japan were far from prepared. TF Smith, an under-strength battalion, was rushed to Korea by the 24th InfDiv in the first days and was easily brushed aside. The two-battalion 34th Infantry Regiment which followed almost immediately suffered a similar defeat.

Defending Pusan

The remnants of five ROK divisions with 45,000 men defended the north side of the 160-mile Pusan perimeter, while the 1st Cav and 24th and 25th InfDivs defended the west side with 30,000 troops. The 2d US InfDiv, the 1st Prov MarBde, and 27th British Infantry Brigade arrived at the end of July and beginning of August. Tank battalions, third battalions for the infantry regiments, artillery batteries, replacements, and supplies were flooding into Pusan.

The marine brigade was rushed to Pusan in response to MacArthur's plea for help. His World War II experience had shown him the value of the marines and he also wanted an amphibious force. MacArthur's plans saw far beyond the immediate defensive battle. The 1st MarDiv, from which the marine brigade had been spawned, was still rebuilding its strength for deployment to Korea. MacArthur had long-range plans for this unit as well. The 7th InfDiv was still in Japan, having been gutted and was being refilled to serve as the Far East Command (FECOM) Reserve. This unit, too, would serve his future plans.

As beaten ROK and US forces plunged south before the North Korean onslaught, MacArthur's mindset was far from defeatist. The contemporary

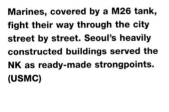

Marines, covered by a M26 tank, fight their way through the city street by street. Seoul's heavily constructed buildings served the NK as ready-made strongpoints. (USMC)

media (and later historians) often describe the Pusan perimeter as a last stand, a defeat in the making, and predicted an "American Dunkirk." In reality, the battered Eighth Army was now positioned to defeat the NK in detail. The Eighth Army had suffered 6,000 US and 70,000 ROK casualties. The ten NK divisions, however, had shrunk to a few thousand exhausted fighters each. The NK had lost almost 58,000 troops and only 40-plus T34 tanks were thought to remain out of 150. Only about 21,000 were veteran troops, the rest being raw recruits whose morale was plummeting. Their supply line, running almost 300 miles from Pyongyang, the NK capital, and through Seoul to the units scattered on a wide front, was over-extended and under UN air and naval attack. Ample air support was provided to the Pusan perimeter from carriers and bases in Japan, only a couple of hundred miles away. The surviving NK now faced 92,000 well supplied and well supported UN troops, some of them fresh.

All that MacArthur felt needed to be done to accommodate a breakout, a counteroffensive to drive the invaders back north, was to sever the fragile NK supply line, but he needed the tools to do it, and it was questionable whether they would be made available. While units and commands worldwide were being combed for troops and equipment there were valid concerns that the whole matter might be a diversion for a Soviet invasion of West Germany. The 82d AbnDiv, though requested by MacArthur, was untouchable as was the 1st InfDiv in Germany. The 82d was all that remained of the General Reserve; other divisions being gutted. The two under-strength marine divisions were needed for other contingencies. MacArthur had requested a marine division, but the JCS said they were unavailable. For what he had in mind he also needed an army division, and none was readily available.

FECOM possessed no amphibious capability. The marine brigade on Guam had been disbanded in April 1949. No viable amphibious training had been undertaken by the divisions in Japan or by any other army division. In late 1949, as a contingency for a Soviet invasion of Japan, joint navy and marine training teams were formed to train one regiment in each of the four divisions for amphibious counter-landings. The program had only just begun at the time of the invasion. The first concept of a flanking amphibious operation on the Korean peninsula was a modest effort involving the 1st Cavalry Division (CavDiv) still in Japan. The amphibious training teams were retasked to provide as much training as possible to the 1st Cav in the short time available. Operation *Bluehearts*, though, degenerated into simply landing the 1st Cav as reinforcements for Pusan.

By any rational assessment the two undermanned, under-equipped, untrained divisions tasked with the Inch'on–Seoul operation were incapable of accomplishing the mission.

The "Old Breed"

MacArthur had immediately asked the Joint Chiefs of Staff (JCS) for a marine division, but had been told none was available. It appears, however, that this decision was made by the JCS without consulting the Navy Department. On June 28 the Commandant of the Marine Corps recommended to the Chief of Naval Operations that a marine unit be committed to Korea, and Commander, Naval Forces, Far East was advised that a Marine Regimental Combat Team (RCT) was available.

Marines carry a wounded comrade across bullet-swept streets in the suburbs of Seoul. Even after an area had been cleared there was still a constant danger from bypassed and infiltrating snipers. (USMC)

So, on July 2, the day TF Smith battalion arrived in Korea, MacArthur, requested a marine RCT[2] accompanied by air support, knowing that the marines could quickly field one. Discussions were also underway to prepare a marine division as a reserve for Korea.

The 1st Provisional Marine Brigade (1st Prov MarBde) was hastily formed at Camp Pendleton, California on July 7 under BGen Edward A. Craig and built around the 5th Marines and Marine Aircraft Group 33 (MAG-33). More than just an RCT, the brigade consisted of a full complement of support units. The 1st MarDiv was gutted to form the brigade and troops were flown in from the 2d MarDiv. The three infantry battalions were each a rifle company short, but third rifle platoons were assembled for the six companies, although they were still each 50 men short. The tank company, trained on M4A3 Shermans, was outfitted with M26 Pershings pulled from storage. The infantrymen were armed with the new 3.5in. bazooka; it was already clear that the 2.36in. was worthless against T34s. MAG-33 was assigned three F4U Corsair fighter squadrons, one night-fighter-equipped, plus an observation squadron with spotter planes and helicopters. The brigade shipped out July 12–14 with over 6,500 personnel. Without benefit of collective training, the brigade was assembled from men of many units, completely re-equipped, embarked, and on its way in a week. While en route to Japan, the brigade's ground element was ordered directly to Pusan because of the deteriorating situation. It arrived on August 2 and was immediately thrown into the perimeter. On the 6th, in conjunction with 25th InfDiv elements, the brigade launched an attack westward to throw the enemy off balance. On the 12th the brigade was ordered to move north to support the 24th InfDiv during the battle of the Naktong. Committed to action on the 17th, the brigade was instrumental in recovering lost ground. The brigade was placed in reserve on the 21st and it received replacements

---

2 A marine or army RCT consisted of a core infantry regiment, 105mm artillery battalion, engineer and medical companies, usually a tank element, other combat support elements as necessary, and small service support elements.

Marine aviation would play an important role in the Inch'on–Seoul Campaign, both carrier- and land-based. This Marine Fighter Squadron 312 "Checkboards" F4U-4B Corsair sits on Kimpo Airfield. (USMC)

and training. As higher headquarters fought over the question of employing the brigade in the planned Inch'on landing, it was returned to the Naktong Bulge on September 1, which had again been overrun. It helped restore the situation and the overall action helped break the back of the final NK offensive to carry the Pusan perimeter. Assembling at Pusan on September 7, the exhausted marines found third companies had arrived for each battalion along with replacements. They also found they were departing Pusan for points unknown. A hurried week was spent re-organizing, incorporating and training replacements, re-equipping, training the attached 1st Korean Marine Corps (KMC) Regiment, and embarking aboard ships. The brigade sailed on the 15th having been formally disbanded and re-incorporated into the 1stMarDiv.

While the 1st Prov MarBde was making history at Pusan, the Marine Corps was frantically preparing the 1st MarDiv to follow. Marine units throughout the corps were stripped of men to fill the division. It contained less than 3,400 troops when the brigade departed and the 1st Marine Aircraft Wing (1st MAW), which would accompany the division, about 2,500. Not only did these two units have to be rebuilt and deployed, but the 2d MarDiv, 2d MAW, and numerous non-divisional units had to be filled. The 129,000 Marine Reservists were immediately mobilized and Marine Security Forces and other branches contributed 50 percent of their personnel. In the first week of August, almost 14,000 regulars and reservists arrived at Camp Pendleton. The first divisional units were scheduled to depart on August 10 and for all practical purposes the units did not exist. The 1st Marines was built from scratch, as were other units. The 2d MarDiv's three artillery battalions were sent from North Carolina; the 1st MarDiv's only artillery battalion was with the brigade. The second regiment would be provided by the 1st Prov MarBde, which would be absorbed into the division. Once pulled from the Pusan perimeter it would be leading the Inch'on assault ten days later. The third regiment, ordered raised on August 10, and other supporting units would come partly from the 2d MarDiv. This regiment, the 7th Marines, would not depart for Korea until September 3. It was built from the 6th Marines which arrived at Pendleton on August 16 with two weak battalions along

The USS *George Clymer* (APA-27) prepares to cast off for Inch'on at Kobe. Landing craft, medium (LCM) can be seen on the aft cargo deck. (USN)

with other 2d MarDiv troops. The 6th's 3d Battalion was afloat in the Mediterranean and would join the regiment in Korea via the Suez Canal. RCT-7 would follow later. What little training time was available was spent on conditioning drills and test-firing weapons.

The 1st MarDiv sailed August 10–22, but it was really only a third of a division, with the 5th Marines already in Korea and the 7th Marines to follow. The supporting battalions had only one or two companies as the others were with RCT-5 and RCT-7. Staff groups were flown ahead to Korea to begin planning and to co-ordinate the division's arrival. The division arrived at Kobe, Japan between August 29 and September 3. Little time remained until the scheduled September 15 Inch'on landing. Individual and amphibious instruction took place aboard ships. Little field training time was granted at Kobe because of the need to undertake additional combat-loading of equipment and supplies, and this was further hampered by a typhoon.

The 1st MarDiv comprised a core of regulars with combat experience, officers and NCOs. Virtually all company commanders and up had seen combat. However, most of the active-duty junior officers, junior NCOs, and enlisted men had no combat experience, while of the reservists, 99 percent of the officers and 77.5 percent of the enlisted were World War II veterans.

A combined arms brigade, where none had existed, had been raised, deployed, and successfully committed to combat in four weeks. A division with only 2,500 troops was filled out, shipped, and conducted an amphibious assault in eight weeks. The fact that these formations were thrown together from scores of units, manned by regulars and reservists who just weeks before were pursuing civilian endeavors, and had been afforded virtually no collective or large unit tactical training can be described as nothing less than a phenomenal feat.

The "Bayonet Division"

In many ways the second division to participate in the Inch'on–Seoul operation was in worse shape than the 1st MarDiv. The 7th InfDiv was headquartered in Sapporo on Hokkaido, the second northernmost of

7th Marines' machine gunners board a transport at Kobe, Japan bound for Inch'on. They are armed with .30 cal M1919A4 light machine guns, and their uniforms and equipment were the same as those worn by their comrades in World War II. (USMC)

the Japanese Home Islands. Like the other three occupation divisions, it was several thousand men under-strength when the war began. The division was severely gutted to fill the other three as they deployed to Korea. Three infantry battalions were broken up as fillers for the 1st CavDiv. Some 1,640 troops were re-assigned to the 24th and 25th InfDivs. The 7th was next tasked to fill the vacuum left by the departing divisions and sent undermanned units throughout Japan to secure the former occupation units' areas. This made any form of unit training impossible. Individual replacements continued to be drawn from the division and its strength fell to 5,000, as did morale.

On July 4 it was decided to employ the 7th for an amphibious operation and it was slowly built up with a target date of August 15. Replacements filtered in and three cadre battalions (officers, NCOs, specialists) were assigned from the 3d InfDiv in the States, with the intent of filling them with replacements; 20 percent of the replacements from the States were ordered to the 7th InfDiv and 30 percent on August 10.

In August the division concentrated in a training area near Yokohama and was promised much in the way of replacements and equipment, but received little. Troops continued to draw off to Pusan. The division now possessed 8,800 troops, less than half its authorized strength of 18,800. The 7th was relieved of occupation duties on July 26. Between August 23 and September 3 all infantry replacements from the States were sent to the 7th and all artillery replacements to the 8th, 5,800 in all. This of course denied replacements to the divisions defending Pusan.

On August 18, less than a month from D-Day, the division was informed that 8,637 replacements were arriving in Yokohama. Organizing transportation, the commander rushed to the port to find completely untrained and often unfit Korean recruits press-ganged off the streets of Pusan. They required delousing, uniforms, equipment, and weapons. They were to be outfitted, trained, and integrated into American units. The language barrier was insurmountable and there were many morale and cultural issues. These Korean Augmentation to the US Army personnel (KATUSA – pronounced "ka-to-sa") were to be incorporated into US units. About 100 were assigned to each rifle company and artillery battery, meaning there were more Koreans than Americans in the units. The 32d Infantry, the division's main participant in the battle, contained 3,110 Americans and 1,802 Koreans. Training continued, but there were serious concerns with regard to the rebuilt division's readiness. To replace the 7th as the FECOM Reserve, the 3d InfDiv arrived on September 16, the day after the Inch'on landing. Including attachments, the 7th deployed with 24,845 troops and was only 1,400 men short.

MacArthur wanted one other army unit for Operation *Chromite*. He requested an RCT from the 82d AbnDiv. The JCS, though, refused to tap the 82d, the nation's only General Reserve unit. The 187th ARCT (Airborne Regimental Combat Team) from the 11th AbnDiv could be sent, but had to be built up and trained. With the prohibition on air-lifting units to Korea, the unit would have to be sea-lifted and would not arrive until October 18.

THE BATTLEGROUND

Geographic and hydrographic characteristics would make the Inch'on landing one of the most difficult ever attempted. Inch'on is situated on the upper west coast of the Republic of Korea, 20 miles west-southwest of Seoul and 30 miles south of the 38th Parallel. Known as Jinsing to the Japanese, and with a prewar population of 250,000, Inch'on sat on a blunt two square mile short peninsula. It was an industrial city and had long served as Seoul's seaport. The coastal terrain was mostly flat, but several small hills rose within the city, the most notable being Cemetery Hill (130ft) and British Consulate Hill (150ft), Hill 117 (384ft), and a forested ridge about 700 yards square, some 500–700yd inland, Observatory Hill (200ft). The inland base of the peninsula was hilly, and the hills rose farther inland until disappearing into the large plain of the

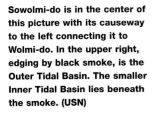

Sowolmi-do is in the center of this picture with its causeway to the left connecting it to Wolmi-do. In the upper right, edging by black smoke, is the Outer Tidal Basin. The smaller Inner Tidal Basin lies beneath the smoke. (USN)

The hills on the northwest side of Seoul were higher and more rugged. The NKs established their main line of resistance across these hills and ridges. In the foreground is a railroad embankment. (USMC)

The Inch'on Railroad Station still burns on D+1 from the naval bombardment it received the day before. (USMC)

Kimpo Peninsula which stretched north with the Yellow Sea on its west side and the Han River estuary on its east.

Wolmi-do (Moon Tip Island) dominated the harbor, being 800yd west off the end of the Inch'on peninsula. The roughly triangular-shaped island measured some 1,000yd each side. Most of the island was occupied by a steep-sided, brush-covered 351-ft hill, known as Radio Hill because of the commercial radio antenna. The island's northeast side and northern tip was occupied by an industrial area. It was also a fishing boat base and tourist attraction with a swimming pool, shops, and restaurants. A 800-yd causeway connected Wolmi-do with the mainland. Another 750-yd causeway jutting south from the west corner was connected to Sowolmi-do, a rocky, hill-like islet with a lighthouse. The two 12-yd wide causeways served as breakwaters enclosing the north and west sides of Inch'on Harbor (Inch'on Hang). The northeast side of the harbor was edged with a waterfront of piers, warehouses, and port facilities. Stone and concrete seawalls (up to 15ft high at high tide) faced the city and port waterfronts, as well as Wolmi-do itself. On the southeast side of the harbor was a large tidal basin, and thrusting out 1,400yd from it was a stone breakwater that defined the south side of the harbor. Port facilities also lined the shore outside the main harbor to the north. On the south side were the Inner and Outer Tidal Basins providing a haven for ships when receding tides would leave them stranded on the mud flats. Near the base of both sides of the peninsula were large salt evaporation pans. The city's streets were a chaotic maze and many buildings were of concrete and masonry construction.

To reach Inch'on from the Yellow Sea, either the western Flying Fish Channel (So Sudo) or the near-shore East Channel (Tong Sudo) had to be negotiated from the southwest, winding through scattered islands, mud banks, rock outcroppings, and strong currents; both routes were 50 miles long and the channels 36–60ft deep. The East Channel ran between Yongdungpo-do and Taebu-do, 15 miles south of Inch'on (Taebu-do was occupied by North Korea). Flying Fish Channel ran north of Yong-hong-do. The two channels converged at Palmi-do, an islet 10 miles from Inch'on. To make matters worse, the fleet would have to make this dangerous approach in darkness to take advantage of the morning high tide. The Flying Fish Channel was selected with fewer hazards. There was no maneuver space in the 2,000–3,500yd channel between Inch'on and Yongjong-do and its fringing 6,000yd wide mud flats to the northwest if the invasion fleet was attacked by air, and even less when the tide ebbed.

Once Inch'on was secured the marines would have to cover 20 miles of ground to reach Seoul on the Inch'on–Seoul Highway, which had a railroad running parallel along it. The ground was comparatively flat, but there were numerous scattered hills affording the North Koreans defensive positions. The low, round-topped hills and ridges had

The north-central section of Seoul with Government House, the capitol, in the upper center. To the right can be seen the Duksoo Imperial Palace. The hills on the city's north side are just off the top of the photograph. (USA)

19

gradually sloped sides and were either bare or partly covered by brush or pine trees. However, there were numerous gullies on the flat ground and hillsides and a few wooded areas offering cover. The level ground consisted of cultivated fields and rice paddies cut by small streams. The area had also been used as a Japanese training ground and was dotted with concrete pillboxes and obstacles, which the North Koreans employed. Ascom City[3], Sosa, and Yongdungp'o lay astride the route. The latter, an industrial suburb, sat on the south side of the Han River opposite Seoul. Between the town and river was a vast sandy flat on which the small Seoul airstrip sat. The main airfield in the area, though, was Kimpo to the northwest of Yongdungp'o and south of the river. The highway and railroad bridges connecting Yongdungp'o and Seoul had been destroyed before the North Koreans took the city. From Yongdungp'o a highway ran south to Suwon and Osan. This was the main North Korean supply route to Pusan and it would also be one of the routes Eighth US Army would take north once it broke out. Ferry crossings were located at Haengju northwest of Seoul, and Sinsa-ri on the city's southeast side, but all the ferries had been destroyed.

The northwest-flowing Han presented an obstacle on the route to Seoul, but the river was slow and only a few hundred yards wide. Its depth though, even far inland, was affected by Yellow Sea tides. While it separated regiments of the 1st MarDiv for part of the operation, the NK never took full advantage of it as a barrier. The marine and army amphibious tractors (amtracs) were invaluable in the crossing of this and other water obstacles.

In 1950 Seoul (Keijo to the Japanese, and still identified as such on maps) was the fifth largest city in Asia, with a population of 680,000. Situated on a bend on the north bank of the Han, Seoul was a relatively modern city with many multistorey concrete and masonry businesses, commercial buildings, and apartment blocks. Among these were the city

---

[3] Ascom City's native name is Taejong-ni. During the US occupation it was developed as the Army Service Command base resulting in "Ascom," the common name used in official histories.

hall, large school complexes, churches, hotels, embassies, Yongsan Railroad Station, Sodaeman Prison, and the ancient Duksoo Imperial Palace. The Japanese had built Government House, the largest concrete building in Asia, in front of the Imperial Palace grounds to obscure it. Government House had served as the Japanese colonial capitol, the Republic of Korea capitol building, and a North Korean strongpoint. In the sprawling suburbs were wooden and masonry dwellings. Hills and ridges were scattered through Seoul and defined its limits. On the north and northwest sides it was overlooked by forested hills. The streets were broad and several railroads ran through the city. Main highways ran northwest to Kaesong, northeast to Uijongbu, and southeast to Ch'ungiu.

The hydrographic characteristics of the Inch'on area were a major issue with invasion planners and higher headquarters. Inch'on experienced the second most drastic tidal changes in the world[4]. At the time of the landing the spring tide would be higher than normal, with 23–33ft tides. A 25ft tide was necessary for small landing craft to reach the seawall. On September 15 there would be a 31.5ft tide, higher than normal. This would provide the 29ft of water required by the Landing Ships, Tank (LST). Only on a few days in the middle of September and October would sufficient depths be available. The morning high tide would be at 0659hrs followed by a low tide that saw the bay empty of water tearing out at 6–7 knots. Evening high tide would be at 1919hrs with a flood rate of 3 knots. When the tide was out any ships remaining in the nearshore bay would be stranded on mud flats, although ships in the channel remained afloat. In case they were stranded, ships were armed with grenades and submachine guns to guard against North Korean infantry attacks across the mud.

Day temperatures were warm, upper 80°F with frequent rain squalls and the skies partly overcast on D-Day. Nights were cool in the low 70°F range. Nightfall was at 1900hrs. The varied terrain would be a challenge to the marines and soldiers involved in this campaign. They would conduct an amphibious landing, fight in large modern cities and crude peasant villages against a well-entrenched enemy; they had to carry out multiple river crossings and face armor attacks on hills, ridges, open plains, and rice paddies.

---

[4] The most drastic tidal changes are found in the Bay of Fundy, Nova Scotia.

CHRONOLOGY

1950

25 June	North Korea (NK) invades the Republic of Korea (ROK) with the backing of the USSR.
27 June	US forces authorized to conduct air and naval operations in support of the ROK south of the 38th Parallel. UN passes resolution authorizing armed force to restore peace. US Reserve forces authorized for call-up.
28 June	Seoul seized by NK. US Seventh Fleet assigned to Naval Forces, Far East.
29 June	Naval blockade of Korea authorized and first US Navy offensive actions occur. Offensive air operations authorized in NK. US ground forces authorized for commitment to ROK in support role.
30 June	US ground forces authorized for commitment to ROK for combat operations.
1 July	US Task Force Smith, deployed by 24th US InfDiv, arrives.
3 July	First UN carrier air strikes executed in NK. Inch'on seized by NK.
5 July	Task Force Smith defeated by NK forces in first US ground action.
7 July	1st Prov MarBde formed for immediate duty in ROK.
12–14 July	1st Prov MarBde departs for ROK.
13 July	Eighth US Army in Korea headquarters formed.
14 July	ROK forces placed under United Nations command.
17 July	ROK forces delegated to Eighth US Army.
2 August	1st Prov MarBde arrives at Pusan.
4 August	Pusan (aka Naktong) perimeter established as UN forces are pushed into the southeast corner of Korea.
8–18 August	Battle of Naktong defeats NK penetration of Pusan perimeter.
10–22 August	1st MarDiv (-) departs for Japan.
15 August	Korean Augmentation to the US Army approved.
23 August	Decision made to land at Inch'on.
26 August	X US Corps activated in Japan.
28 August	X US Corps issues Operation Order 1 for Inch'on.
30 August	Naval Forces Far East issues Operation Plan 108-50 assigning JTF7 the mission of seizing Inch'on.
31 Aug–19 Sep	Second battle of the Naktong.
1 September	Reconnaissance of Inch'on Harbor and approaches commence.
3 September	Korean Marine Regiment attached to 1st MarDiv.
4 September	1st MarDiv issues Operation Order 2-50 for Inch'on. JTF7 and TF90 orders are issued concurrently.
5–12 September	1st MarDiv departs Japan for Inch'on.
13 September	1st Prov MarBde departs Pusan for Inch'on.
10 September	Preliminary air attacks commence in Inch'on area.
11 September	JTF7 formally activated to execute landing.

NK prisoners are marched past a battered T34. Prisoners were often stripped because of the fear of concealed grenades and pistols. (USMC)

13 September	1st Prov MarBde re-absorbed into 1st MarDiv and departs Pusan for Inch'on. Pre-landing bombardment commences.
15 September	1st MarDiv lands at Inch'on.
16 September	Inch'on secured.
16–22 September	Eighth US Army breaks out of Pusan perimeter.
17 September	NK counterattacks outside of Inch'on. Ascom City and Kimpo Airfield secured. 7th InfDiv arrives at Pusan. 7th Marines departs Japan for Inch'on.
18 September	7th InfDiv begins debarking at Inch'on.
20 September	5th Marines cross Han River. NK counterattacks outside Yongdungp'o.
21 September	Yongdungp'o secured. 7th Marines arrive at Inch'on.
22–24 September	Approaches to Seoul secured and NK main defenses penetrated.
24 September	1st Marines cross Han River into southwest Seoul.
25 September	1st MarDiv launches main attack into west Seoul. RCT-32 crosses Han River into south Seoul.
26 September	Eighth Army elements from Pusan and X Corps troops from Inch'on link up at Osan.
27 September	Seoul liberated by US and ROK forces.
28 Sep–3 Oct	UN forces continue to drive north from Seoul and secures Uijongbu.
29 September	Seoul re-established as capital of ROK.
30 September	ROK forces cross the 38th Parallel.
4 October	China decides to intervene in Korea.
5 October	Inch'on–Seoul Campaign completed.
6–8 October	X Corps assembles at Inch'on and begins embarkation for Wonsan.
9 October	First US forces cross the 38th Parallel.
25 October	China commences surprise offensive into NK.

1951

4 January	Seoul evacuated and falls to Chinese.
5 January	Inch'on evacuated.
14 March	Seoul liberated by ROK forces.

OPPOSING COMMANDERS

AMERICAN COMMANDERS

There is no disputing that **General of the Army Douglas MacArthur (USA)** was the motivating force behind Operation *Chromite*. It was his willpower and certainty that this was the best course of action that drove him to force the operation through, often in virtual defiance of his superiors and the counsel of his subordinates. Arguably the most controversial general in American history, he was constantly aware of his place in that history. MacArthur was born in Arkansas in 1880 and entered the Military Academy in 1900. He was commissioned in the engineers in 1903 and served in the Philippines. Between 1904 and 1912 he was an aide to Commander, Pacific Division, served in an engineer unit, attended the Engineer School, was aide to President Theodore Roosevelt, and an instructor. From 1913–17 he served on the General Staff and took part in the 1914 Vera Cruz Expedition. He served in France from 1917–18 as chief of staff of the 42d Division and commanded the division during the Sedan Offensive. He was Superintendent of the Military Academy from 1919–22. He commanded the Manila District from 1922–23 and then on various corps staffs through 1930. From 1930–35 he was Chief of Staff of the Army. He personally directed the suppression of the bonus marchers in Washington (the 1932 gathering of World War I veterans demanding immediate compensation of their war service), an unsavory task for which he received much criticism. In 1935 he became the military adviser to the government of the Philippines.

VIPs visit the Inch'on beachhead, D+1. From left to right: LtGen Lemuel C. Sheperd, Jr. (Fleet Marine Force, Pacific), ViceAdm Arthur D. Struble (JTF7/Seventh Fleet), Gen MacArthur, MajGen Courtney Whitney (Chief of Government Section, FECOM) and BGen Edwin K. Wright (Assistant G3, FECOM). (USN)

MacArthur retired from active duty in 1937, but continued in his position with the Philippine government. In 1941, with war on the horizon, he was restored to active duty and took command of US Army forces in the Far East. Overseeing the initial defense of the Philippines, MacArthur was ordered to Australia. There he commanded the Southwest Pacific Area and then was designated the Supreme Allied Commander to execute the invasion of Japan and its occupation. He presided over Japan's surrender and was instrumental in the country's reconstruction. As such, he held the titles of Supreme Allied Commander, Japan; Commanding General, Far East Command; and Commander-in-Chief, Allied Forces, Far East, and in July 1950, Commander-in-Chief, UN Command. His management of the defense of Korea was controversial and his outright defiance of President Truman resulted in his dismissal from command in April 1951. Going gracefully into retirement at age 71, he was without question one of the most influential men of the era in Asian and Pacific affairs. He died in 1964.

ViceAdm Arthur D. Struble (USN) was born in Oregon in 1894, entered the Naval Academy in 1911, and was commissioned in 1915. He served aboard cruisers and destroyers and was assigned as an instructor to the Naval Academy from 1921–23. He next served on the USS *California* until assigned to the Battle Fleet staff in 1925. This was followed by two tours in the Navy Department, then the USS *New York*, followed by a cruiser, and additional fleet staff assignments. He was executive officer of the USS *Arizona* from 1940–41 and commanded a light cruiser in the Pacific. In 1942 he served in the Office of the Chief of Naval Operations, went to Britain in 1943, and was on the Naval Forces, Europe staff responsible for the Normandy landing. Returning to the Pacific in 1944, he took command of the Seventh Fleet's ("MacArthur's Navy") amphibious force and conducted numerous landings throughout the Philippines. After the war he commanded the Pacific Fleet's mine force to clear mined areas throughout the region. This was followed by command of Amphibious Force, Pacific Fleet until 1949. He was promoted to vice admiral during that tour and then served as the Deputy Chief of Naval Operations until 1950, at which time he assumed command of the Seventh Fleet based in the Philippines. As such he commanded the naval forces of the Inch'on and Wonsan landings until taking over the First Fleet in March 1951. He next headed the US naval and military delegations to the UN Military Staff Committee. From 1955 he commanded the Eastern Sea Frontier and the Atlantic Reserve Fleet until his retirement the following year, at which time he was promoted to admiral. He died in 1983.

MajGen Edward ("Ned") M. Almond's (USA) assignment as X Corps commander has been considered by some as unfortunate as he had absolutely no experience with amphibious operations. His military career to this point, while impressive on the surface, had been somewhat lackluster. Born in Virginia in 1892 and raised with a strong reverence for the Civil War's legacy and family bonds, he attended the Virginia Military Institute graduating in 1915. He was commissioned in the US Army in 1917 and assigned as a 4th Division machine-gun company commander. Wounded on his first day of combat, he later commanded a machine-gun battalion for one month of combat. He served as an Reserve Officer Training Corps instructor until attending the Infantry School in 1923, and then was an instructor there until attending the Command and General Staff School from 1928–30. His only between-the-wars troop duty was as a battalion commander of the Philippine Scouts. In 1933 he attended the Army War College and then served on the Army General Staff for the next five years. Understanding the necessity for joint warfare, he attended the Air Corps Technical School and then the Navy War College. When the war began he was assigned as the assistant division commander of the 93d InfDiv (Colored). He had been selected for this assignment because of his reputation as a strong disciplinarian, his extensive military instructor experience, and service with native troops; his Southern background was also considered a desirable trait for commanders of African-American units. It was a duty neither he nor many other white officers relished. He had only limited battalion command time and had never commanded or even been assigned to regimental or brigade staffs. Before long he received command of the 92d InfDiv (Colored), which deployed to Italy in 1944. The unit's performance was less than successful, with some units breaking and running, others were spiritless; a few performed well. Withdrawn from combat, it underwent retraining, but when again recommitted at the beginning of 1945 its performance was still poor and two black regiments were withdrawn and replaced by white and Japanese-American regiments. Almond's ability to lead the division was never questioned and he received no blame. He suffered another form of tragedy losing his son and son-in-law in combat, a powerful blow to one steeped in Southern family traditions. He was given command of the 2d InfDiv scheduled for redeployment for the invasion of Japan, but the war was over. In early 1946 he was offered the position of military attaché to the USSR, but he declined, asserting that he despised Communism and the conduct of the Red Army in the war. Almond understood that his command of a lackluster black division and his rejection of the USSR duty may have damaged his career. He was assigned to MacArthur's staff as the G-1 (personnel). His hard work and reputation for exactness caught MacArthur's attention and in February 1949 he became the FECOM Chief of Staff. In the first traumatic months of the Korean War Almond worked tirelessly. With plans underway for Inch'on and the formation of a new corps to oversee the operation, MacArthur promised X Corps to Ned Almond and he assumed command on August 26. His command, though, would not be without its problems. Almond was frequently over-demanding and even untrusting of his subordinate commanders, and some of the plans he proposed were far-fetched. He was often impatient and arrogant. His G-3 stated, "He could precipitate a crisis on a desert island with nobody else around." He was promoted to lieutenant general on February 15, 1951 and commanded X Corps until July 15. His last assignment was Commandant of the Army War College. He retired in 1953 as a lieutenant general and passed away in 1979.

MajGen Oliver P. Smith's (USMC) early career was less impressive than Almond's. He was commissioned in the Army Reserve, but transferred to the Marine Corps in 1917. He missed the corps' glory in France, serving instead on Guam. Smith was born in Texas in 1893 and worked his way through the University of California. Through the 1920s he served in marine barracks, aboard the USS *Texas*, on the Marine Corps staff, and in Haiti in the gendarmerie. From 1931–30 he attended the

Field Officers' Course and then was an instructor at Quantico. He spent two years at France's prestigious *Ecole Supérieur la da Guerre* and then went back to Quantico as an instructor. He was commanding 1st Battalion, 6th Marines when World War II broke out and he led the unit to Iceland. Upon return he again served on the Marine Corps staff and departed for the Pacific in early 1944 to command the 5th Marines on New Britain with the 1st MarDiv. He then served as assistant division commander on Peleliu and on Okinawa as a deputy chief of staff in Tenth Army. His postwar assignments included commanding the Marine Corps Schools at Quantico, at which time he was dual-billeted as commander, 1st Special MarBde, a Caribbean contingency force, and then as chief of staff and later as commandant of Headquarters, Marine Corps. Smith took command of the 1st MarDiv on July 26, 1950 commanding it until April 27, 1951. From February 25–March 5, 1951 he served as the temporary commander of IX Corps after the commander died of a heart attack, but was quickly replaced by an army officer. Smith was a temperate, religious man, who seldom showed anger or swore. He was especially known for not risking his men needlessly. Regardless, the press sometimes confused him with Gen "Howlin' Mad" Holland M. Smith, a personality who was the opposite in every way of "O.P." Smith. Considered slow and plodding by some, his studious quietness led to another nickname, "the Professor." Regardless of his amiable nature, his relationship to Almond was tumultuous. After Korea, Smith commanded Camp Pendleton, California then Fleet Marine Force, Atlantic. He retired in 1955 and died on Christmas Day, 1977.

MajGen Oliver P. Smith, 1st MarDiv (left), discusses the operation with MajGen Edward M. Almond (X Corps). Over Almond's shoulder is MajGen Field Harris (1st MAW). The relationship between Smith and Almond can best be described as fiery. (USMC)

MajGen David G. Barr (USA) was another Southern officer, having been born in Alabama in 1895. He served in the 1st Division in World War I and received the Silver Star for valor. Regardless, he was never considered a good combat leader or field commander. The highest peacetime command he held was as company commander. He was an excellent staff officer though, and having graduated from the Command and General Staff College and Army War College he served as the chief of staff of several high commands during World War II: Armored Force from 1942–43; North African Theater of Operations 1944 where he was promoted to major general early in the year; and Sixth Army Group in France 1944–45. From 1945–48 he was chief of personnel of the Army Ground Forces. He was given command of the 7th InfDiv in 1949 mainly based on his seniority. The phone call that had offered MajGen Almond the military attaché assignment to the USSR had been made by Barr, and it was he who subsequently assigned him to MacArthur's GHQ. Barr was now under Almond's command and disagreements were common. It is said that he was probably more qualified to command a division when he took over the 7th, than Almond when he took command of the ill-starred 92d. While he was two years junior in rank to Almond, he actually had almost as much commissioned service time as his superior. Like Almond, Barr was a proficient staffer, but he was quiet and reserved compared to the more dynamic Almond. He did seem to lack complete self-confidence, and, because of his honesty when reporting his division's faults, he made himself easy prey to Almond. He and his staff never tended to question orders from Almond's headquarters, no matter how problematic they might be, but simply drove on and suffered the consequences. His G-3 said of him, "I admired and respected General

Barr, although he was not what I would term a combat officer or troop commander type. He was courtly, kind, friendly, very intelligent, capable, and, I think, aware of his shortcomings." He left the 7th InfDiv on January 26, 1951 to become commandant of the Armor School until he retired in 1952. He died in 1970.

The other key leadership of X Corps' divisions follows:

1st Marine Division (Reinforced)

Assistant Division Commander	BGen Edward A. Craig
Chief of Staff	Col Gregon A. Williams
1st Marines	Col Lewis B. Puller
5th Marines	LtCol Raymond L. Murray
7th Marines	Col Homer L. Litzenberg, Jr.
11th Marines (Artillery)	Col James H. Brower
1st KMC Regiment	Col Shin Hyen Jun
1st Marine Aircraft Wing	MajGen Field Harris
1st Combat Support Group	Col J.S. Cook
2d Engineer Special Brigade	Col Joseph J. Twitty (USA)

7th Infantry Division

Assistant Division Commander	BGen Henry I. Hodes
Chief of Staff	Col Louis T. Heath
17th Infantry Regiment	Col Herbert B. Powell
31st Infantry Regiment	Col Richard P. Overshine*
32d Infantry Regiment	Col Charles E. Beauchamp
17th ROK Infantry Regiment	Col Paik In Yup
Division Artillery	BGen Homer W. Kiefer

* Relieved October 5, replaced by Col Allen D. MacLean.

NORTH KOREAN COMMANDERS

Virtually no information exists on North Korean commanders at Inch'on and Seoul. Only the names of a few are known and no biographical information is available. Most NK officers, even many of the junior officers, were combat-experienced. One of the few known commanders was MajGen Wol Ki Chan who commanded the 25th Rifle Brigade in Seoul. Another is 40-year-old BGen Wan Yong, commanding the 1st Air Force Division at Kimpo Airfield. Nothing else is known of either other than they were Chinese-trained.

Among them were former anti-Japanese guerrillas, Japanese-raised colonial police, former conscripted Korean officers and soldiers who had served in the Imperial Japanese Army and the Japanese puppet Manchukuo Army in North China, some 40,000 Korean Volunteer Army troops who fought with the Chinese Communist People's Liberation Army against the nationalists in eight Chinese divisions, and the Yi Homg-gwang Detachment. Many of the men of these units had deserted from the Japanese Army. The Korean Volunteer Army attempted to return to Korea in 1945, but the Soviet occupiers would not permit it. In 1946–47 they were allowed to return and incorporated into the fledgling KPA. The Yi Homg-gwang continued to serve with the Chinese until 1948 when it, too, returned to Korea. Some 2,500 Koreans who had fought at Stalingrad with the Red Army were also sent to North Korea. Most of these men had been Soviet citizens; a large Korean community resided in Russia. The Korean guerrilla forces had been trained by the Soviets to fight the Japanese through World War II. Much of the higher leadership of the KPA came from the guerrillas. They had been well indoctrinated by the Soviets and their return was permitted in 1945. Kim Il Sung, the Premier and Supreme Commander-in-Chief, came from this source.

The Pyongyang Military Academy was established in 1945 along with three security officer training schools, and for the next three years the main focus was on training a large cadre of officers rather than actually raising an army. From 1946–49 thousands of NK troops were sent to China, both to aid the Chinese fighting the Nationalists, and to gain even more combat experience. The officers, many with minimal education and unfamiliar with the world outside North Korea and the places where they fought, were under total Communist control. Besides military skills and tactics, they were saturated with anti-capitalist, anti-democratic, anti-South Korean, anti-American, anti-United Nations, and anti-Western propaganda. Many North Koreans were sent to the USSR for technical training and the KPA was backed by thousands of Soviet advisers. Tactics focused on the unrelenting offensive with the sole goal of conquering South Korea. Discipline was strict and harsh. Failure was unacceptable and those not giving their all or violating regulations were expected to condemn themselves in self-confession sessions before unit members. Officers could be banished to "re-education" (penal) units and possibly returned to combat units as enlisted men. The Geneva Convention was scorned. Many prisoners and ROK government officials were executed. Surviving prisoners were treated brutally, while many ROKA prisoners were re-armed and forced to fight for the KPA. NK commanders were almost as merciless with their own soldiers. They had no reservations about committing them to near suicidal attacks with little hope of obtaining their objectives.

Regardless of who they were individually, a great many of the North Korean officers at Inch'on and Seoul had gained combat experience fighting against the Nationalist Chinese and to a lesser extent the Japanese. They were used to austere military life, harsh discipline, and had served mostly in the field. They knew their weapons, were used to Spartan diets and uncomfortable living conditions in the field. They were totally dedicated to winning the Fatherland Liberation War at whatever cost.

OPPOSING ARMIES

UN FORCES

The various armed forces defending the Republic of Korea were under United Nations' control. When 53 of the nations comprising the UN General Assembly voted to intervene in Korea, 15 vowed to commit ground forces. At the time of the Inch'on landing, though, few non-US forces had arrived. The ROK itself was not a member of the UN, but its armed forces were placed under UN control on July 14 and directly under Eighth Army control on the 17th. Gen MacArthur was additionally named Commander-in-Chief, UN Command on July 8. The Inch'on–Seoul Campaign would be conducted mostly by US forces. Two ROK regiments and a few small craft would participate along with 20 Commonwealth warships.

The General Headquarters, UN Command was one and the same with the GHQ, Far East Command, headquartered in the Dai-Ichi Building in Tokyo. The two commands were formally merged on July 24 as FEC/UNC. This same staff also served Supreme Commander, Allied Powers in Japan and Commander-in Chief, Allied Forces, Far East – Gen MacArthur.

FECOM controlled three major US operational commands: Eighth US Army, the ground forces; Naval Forces, Far East (NAVFE); and the Far East Air Forces (FEAF). NAVFE, under Adm C. Turner Joy, consisted of a large number of specialized task forces and groups. The Seventh Fleet (TF70) sailing from the Philippines was assigned to NAVFE on July 28 and became its main operating force. All UN and ROK naval elements were under the huge fleet. FEAF, commanded by Gen George E. Stratemeyer, consisted of the Fifth Air Force in Japan, Thirteenth Air Force in the Philippines, and Twentieth Air Force on Okinawa.

As with any large-scale joint amphibious operation, the *Chromite* command structure was complex, involving US Army, Navy, Marine Corps, and Air Force elements. X Corps, rather than being assigned to Eighth Army as other FECOM ground forces, was directly under MacArthur's control.

Commander-in-Chief, Far East/UN Command	**Gen Douglas MacArthur**
Commander, Naval Forces, Far East	ViceAdm C. Turner Joy
Commander, Joint Task Force 7	ViceAdm Arthur D. Struble
Commander, Attack Force (TF90)	RearAdm James H. Doyle
Commander, Amphibious Group 1	RearAdm James H. Doyle
Commanding General, X US Corps (TF92)	MajGen Edward D. Almond
Commanding General, 1st Marine Division	MajGen Oliver P. Smith
Commanding General, 7th Infantry Division	MajGen David G. Barr

1st Marines troops head for Beach Blue on the southeast side of Inch'on aboard LVT(3)C amphibian tractors. They pass LSTs awaiting their turn to beach. (USMC)

Joint Task Force 7

JTF7 was built within the Seventh Fleet, with its commander doubling as JTF7 commander. This joint amphibious force controlled the entire operation. It was organized into the Attack Force (TF90), Blockade and Covering Force (TF91), Landing Force (X Corps – TF92), Patrol and Reconnaissance Force (TF99), Fast Carrier Force (TF77), and Service Squadron (TF79).

Some 261 vessels were assigned to the operation, the largest naval force since World War II and also the largest amphibious operation of the Korean War: 194 US, 15 ROK, 12 British, three Australian, two New Zealand, and one French. Among this armada were four aircraft carriers, two escort carriers, six cruisers, 33 destroyers, five assault transports, 15 assault cargo ships, 32 transports and cargo ships, 15 frigates, three destroyer-transports, two amphibious command ships, three landing ships, dock; three landing ships, medium (rocket) (LSM[R]); many small craft such as minesweepers, tugs, etc.; and dozens of auxiliaries. As for landing craft, there were 85 landing ships, tank (LST)[5]; 20 landing ships, utility (LSU), 70 landing craft, mechanized (LCM), almost 200 landing craft, vehicle and personnel (LCVP), and almost 200 landing vehicles, tracked (LVT – amtracs).

X US Corps

X Corps ("Ten Corps") had been activated in May 1942 at Ft Sherman, Texas. It subsequently served on New Guinea, Leyte, and other southern Philippines islands. It was de-activated in Japan in January 1946 after conducting occupation duty. The corps was re-activated in Tokyo on 26 August 1950 from the GHQ FECOM Special Plans Staff (aka "Force X") with MajGen "Ned" Almond commanding. Chief of Staff was MajGen Clark L. ("Nick") Ruffner who headed a hastily thrown together staff with virtually no amphibious experience. Other than the small Force X core, the staff had no opportunity to train together. X Corps was created specially for the Inch'on landing as the JTF7 Landing Force – TF92. Assigned the 1st MarDiv and 7th InfDiv, the Corps also received other units, too. Corps troops were assembled from units in Japan and others

---

[5] 32 LSTs were crewed by Japanese and were on loan to the Shipping Control Administration, Japan to replace the huge numbers of inter-coastal ships lost during the war which were vital to ensure the country's recovery and development. The use of these Japanese-manned ships was of questionable legality.

sent from the States: 2d Engineer Special Brigade (an amphibious support unit), 5th Artillery Group with three battalions (two 155mm, one AAA), 6th Quartermaster Group, 60th Ordnance Group, plus engineer combat and construction, signal, transportation, and medical battalions plus many smaller support units, all intended for Eighth Army, but diverted to X Corps; in all, 69,450 troops.

After the Inch'on–Seoul Campaign, X Corps remained under FECOM control and conducted the unopposed Wonsan landing on the upper North Korean east coast in October. This was followed by the Chosin Reservoir Campaign and the Corps' subsequent evacuation from Hungnam. The Corps was assigned to Eighth Army after this, December 26, 1950. It operated in the eastern portion of the line for the remainder of the war. The US and ROK divisions assigned to X Corps constantly changed throughout the war. X Corps left Korea in September 1954 and was inactivated at Ft Riley, Kansas on April 27, 1955.

1st Marine Division (Reinforced)
The 1st MarDiv had been raised in February 1941 from the 1st MarBde at Guantánamo Bay, Cuba. It had fought on Guadalcanal, America's first amphibious landing in World War II, in late 1942. The "Old Breed" then secured a lodgement on Cape Gloucester, New Britain fighting there from late 1943 into 1944. The division next landed on Peleliu in 1944, then on Okinawa in the spring of 1945. Tasked with the invasion of Japan, the division instead conducted occupation duty in North China from September 1945 to June 1947. It redeployed to Camp Pendleton where it remained until 1950. Except for a two-and-a-half month stint with IX Corps in early 1951, the 1st Mar Div remained with X Corps until March 1952 fighting in eastern Korea. One of its more notable battles was at Chosin Reservoir. From then on it served under I Corps in western ROK until it returned to Camp Pendleton between February and April 1955. No overseeing marine force headquarters was established in Korea. Instead, Commander, 1st MarDiv (Reinforced) doubled as the senior marine commander in the country to include responsibility for the 1st MAW.

The 1st MarDiv was organized under the 1947 table of organization plus augmentation. In 1950 the Marine Corps no longer possessed a corps-level echelon providing support and services to subordinate divisions. A small number of non-divisional support units were under the Fleet Marine Force, Pacific and Atlantic, but a deployable corps-level headquarters did not exist. These units, which included armored amphibian tractor, engineer, and artillery battalions, could be attached to the Marine Corps' two divisions. For this reason the marine division possessed more organic support units than in World War II. These included amphibian tractor, engineer, medical, motor transport, ordnance, shore party, service, and signal battalions, significantly larger units than found in army divisions. An armored amphibian tractor battalion and a second motor transport battalion were attached along

Covered by the eight 5in. guns of the USS *De Haven* (DD-727) LCVPs carrying RCT-5 head for Beach Red near the upper right of the photograph. (USN)

The marines pioneered the use of helicopters in Korea, using them for reconnaissance, artillery spotting, and medical evacuation. They proved extremely valuable in allowing commanders to maintain contact with their widespread units. Here a Sikorsky HO3S-1 lifts off. (USMC)

A marine fire team returns sniper fire. The fire team, of which there were three per rifle squad, was led by a corporal with an automatic rifleman, an assistant automatic rifleman, and a rifleman, all with .30 cal M1 rifles except the automatic rifleman, who carried a .30cal M1918A2 BAR. (USMC)

with numerous smaller units. The 1st Combat Support Group (Medium) was also attached. which included headquarters, maintenance, supply, support, and truck companies plus smaller detachments.

The division's three infantry regiments had a full strength of 3,902 men. It had a 281-man headquarters and service company, a 140-man mortar company with 12 x 4.2in. M2 mortars, a 112-man antitank company with 12 x 75mm M20 recoilless rifles and 5 x M26 tanks, and three 1,123-man infantry battalions. Each battalion had a headquarters company, a weapons company with a platoon of 4 x 81mm M1 mortars, two platoons with 4 x .30cal M1917A1 heavy machine-guns, and an assault platoon with 18 x 3.5in. bazookas; and three rifle companies with a headquarters, a mortar section of 3 x 60mm M2s, a machine-gun platoon with 6 x .30cal M1919A4 light machine guns, and three rifle platoons. Platoons had a headquarters and three 13-man rifle squads, each with three .30cal M1918A2 Browning automatic rifles (BAR). Rifle companies were designated A–C in the 1st battalion, D–F in the 2d, and

G-I in the 3d. The weapons companies were not lettered, but identified as, for example, Weapons Company, 1st Battalion.

The 11th Marines, the artillery regiment, had three battalions of 105mm howitzers and one, the 4th, of 155mm howitzers. Each battalion had a headquarters and service battery, and three six-tube batteries. Attached was Battery C, 1st 4.5in. Rocket Battalion, with 12 x 4.5in. T66E2 24-tube rocket launchers. The 1st Tank Battalion had a headquarters and service company and three tank companies with 15 90mm gun-armed M26 Pershing tanks. The 1st Amphibian Tractor Battalion was equipped with LVT(3)C amtracs. The Army's attached Company A, 56th Amphibious Tractor Battalion had LVT(A)5 75mm howitzer-armed amphibious tanks.

Both the 5th Marines, arriving from Pusan, and the 7th Marines, en route from the States and the Mediterranean, were supplemented by companies detached from divisional support battalions to form Regimental Combat Teams (RCTs). The battalions were also reinforced with detachments from regiment and division to form Battalion Landing Teams (BLT). The 1st MarDiv was additionally reinforced by the 1st KMC Regiment and various army units.

7th Infantry Division

The 7th InfDiv had been re-activated (it had served in World War I) at Ft Ord, California, on July 1, 1940 in the regular army. It first received desert training and was initially organized as a motorized division, (although it never received the necessary trucks) and then underwent amphibious training with the marines. It seized Attu Island in the Aleutians in 1943 having received no cold-weather training. Part of the division secured unoccupied Kiska. The "Bayonet Division" seized Kwajalein in 1944, followed by landings on Leyte and then Okinawa in 1945. From 1945–49 the division pulled occupation duty in South Korea until it was withdrawn in phases to Japan. There it continued occupation duty on the northern island of Hokkaido having replaced the 11th AbnDiv. The 17th Infantry would initially serve as the Eighth Army Floating Reserve off Pusan and would depart Japan on September 6.

The table of organization for the infantry division dated from 1948. Division troops included medium tank and engineer combat battalions and a reconnaissance company. This last unit was equipped with M8 and M20 armored cars, M24 light tanks, half-tracks, and machine-gun jeeps. Divisional special troops formed a medical battalion, plus signal, ordnance maintenance, quartermaster, military police, and replacement companies. The tank companies had 20 M26 tanks. The division artillery was organized and armed as the marine artillery regiment, except for the addition of an anti-aircraft artillery battalion of four batteries, each with 8 x twin 40mm M19 and 8 x quad .50cal self-propelled AA guns. Only one battery participated in the operation, however.

On the surface the three infantry regiments were similar to their marine counterparts, but there were many differences. The army regiment had more supporting units to include a 285-man headquarters and headquarters company, a 190-man heavy mortar company with 8 x 4.2in. mortars, a 186-man service company, and a 214-man medical company. Although authorized a tank company (148 men, 22 tanks), the 7th InfDiv had none. The three 917-man infantry battalions had a 119-man headquarters and headquarters company, a 165-man heavy weapons company with a machine gun platoon of four each M1917A1 heavy and M1919A6 light machine guns (with crews to man only four), recoilless rifle platoon with 4 x 75mm rifles, and a mortar platoon with 4 x 81mm. A battalion's three rifle companies had a headquarters and a weapon platoon, with 3 x 57mm recoilless rifles and three 60mm mortars. The three rifle platoons had three nine-man rifle squads, each with a BAR, plus a weapons squad with a light machine gun and a 3.5in. bazooka. The regimental headquarters had a jeep-mounted intelligence and reconnaissance platoon and the battalions a similar section (marine regiments did not have organic reconnaissance elements). Companies were designated A–D in the 1st battalion, E–H in the 2d, and I–M (no "J") in the 3d. Companies D, H, and M were heavy weapons. Regimental companies were designated, for example, Service Company, 32d Infantry.

While the earliest US Army units to arrive in Korea were armed with the 2.36in. bazooka, which was ineffective against T34 tanks, the 1st MarDiv and 7th InfDiv arrived with the 3.5in. "super bazooka" at company level. They still had 2.36in. bazookas assigned to headquarters and support units for antitank "defense." Contrary to popular misconception, the 3.5in. was already in limited production, but had not yet been issued to divisions in the Far East.

Republic of Korea units

Two ROK units participated in the campaign. The 1st KMC Regiment was attached to the 1st MarDiv as a third regiment in the absence of the en route 7th Marines. The KMC had been established in April 1945 from selected naval personnel and advised by US Marines who instilled their *esprit de corps.* The unit had conducted raids on the west coast operating from Cheju Island where it had conducted anti-guerrilla operations. It arrived in Pusan on the 5th. It was armed with Japanese weapons, khaki uniforms, and contained many partly trained recruits. Eighth Army re-armed and uniformed the unit prior to its shipping out for Inch'on. Only one range-firing session was allowed to train them in the use of their

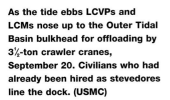

As the tide ebbs LCVPs and LCMs nose up to the Outer Tidal Basin bulkhead for offloading by 3½-ton crawler cranes, September 20. Civilians who had already been hired as stevedores line the dock. (USMC)

Troops of the ROKA 17th Infantry Regiment move into the east side of Seoul. Three-man teams carry .30cal M1917A1 heavy and M1919A4 light machine guns still fitted to tripods on their shoulders Japanese-style. (USMC)

new weapons. The KMC would mainly provide rear area security and mop-up, increasing its experience. Some battalions were to play a more active role.

One ROKA unit was attached to the 7th InfDiv in the form of the 17th Infantry Regiment (Separate), aka Seoul Regiment. It was attached to the Capital Division, but then pulled out of Pusan to participate in the Inch'on–Seoul Campaign, initially to replace the 7th InfDiv's own detached 17th Infantry. Its inclusion in the operation was essential to allow ROK involvement in the liberation of their capital, but was mainly used for rear security and mop-up.

NORTH KOREAN FORCES

Korean People's Army units committed to Inch'on–Seoul were often simply ad hoc elements detached from their parent units. Others were incomplete units with elements detached elsewhere, or under-strength owing to previous combat or the re-assignment of personnel to battered units fighting on at Pusan. Standard tables of organization were meaningless. As Inch'on and Seoul were deep in the enemy's rear and the NK did not expect a major landing, many of the units encountered were security and support units. Their commitment was often piecemeal, with units constantly arriving from the north, east, and south.

While units were incomplete and undermanned, the standard KPA rifle division[6] is examined to provide an understanding of unit organization. At full strength, rifle divisions numbered 11,000–12,000 troops. Those fighting at Pusan were down to 3,000–5,000 men. Divisional troops included antitank (12 x 14.5mm AT rifles, 4 x 45mm AT guns), AA (12 x 14.5mm machine guns), engineer, signal, information and training, and medical battalions plus reconnaissance and transport companies, company-size supply section, and veterinary unit. The artillery regiment

6 The terms "rifle" and "infantry" were used interchangeably by the UN to identify KPA units.

Armed with a M2-2 flamethrower, a member of a battalion assault platoon burns out an NK bunker on Wolmi-do. (USMC)

had two light artillery battalions with 76.2mm guns and a heavy battalion with 122mm howitzers. Battalions had three four-tube batteries. Some divisions had a battalion of 36–45 SU76 self-propelled 76.2mm guns; a few were encountered in Seoul.

The three 2,500-man infantry regiments had a headquarters, submachine gun, signal, mortar (6 x 120mm), artillery (4 x 76.2mm howitzers), and AT (6 x 14.5mm AT rifles, 4 x 45mm AT guns) companies. The three 650-man rifle battalions had headquarters and mortar (9 x 82mm mortars, 2 x 45mm AT guns) companies, and three 150-man rifle companies. Rifle companies had three 45-man rifle platoons of four sections (squads) each with a light machine gun. The weapons platoon had four 60mm mortars and four heavy machine guns.

KPA rifle brigades typically had four or five rifle battalions, an artillery battalion, and minimal service units. NK "marine" units were assigned to the Korean People's Navy for base security and coastal defense. They had no offensive amphibious mission. The various security units were light infantry with minimal crew-served weapons.

The 2,000-man 226th Marine Regiment and a couple of batteries of 2d Battalion, 918th Coast Artillery Regiment were responsible for the defense of Inch'on. The latter was armed with eight 76.2mm field guns, all on Wolmi-do, along with some light AT guns; some 400 troops from both units defended Wolmi-do. The marine regiment had defensive positions edging the seawalls and covering the harbor's piers and other possible landing sites. Other positions were located on Cemetery, Observatory, and British Consulate hills and other high ground in the city. The regimental 120mm mortar company was located on Cemetery Hill. Four abandoned 120mm mortars and four 76.2mm guns were found on the Munhang Peninsula south of Seoul.

A typical ad hoc unit was the "1st Air Force Division" defending Kimpo Airfield, a division in name only. It comprised:

107th Security Regiment
226th Marine Regiment (survivors from Inch'on)

2d Battalion, 1st Regiment
3d Company, 1st Battalion, 1st Regiment
877th Air Force Unit (400 men, unknown composition/function)
1st and 3d Companies, Engineer Battalion, Fighter Regiment
Finance Company, 3d Technical Battalion
Supply company

The 4,000–5,000-man 25th Rifle Brigade defending Seoul consisted of a rifle, 120mm mortar, artillery, engineer, and four machine-gun battalions. The 87th Regiment, 9th Rifle Division had been left in Seoul when the rest of the division was sent to Pusan. The 9th had been raised in early July from border constabulary troops. The largest KPA formation to fight in the campaign was the recently raised 18th Rifle Division, en route to Pusan from Ch'orwon when the landing occurred. It consisted of the 20th, 22d, and 24th Rifle Regiments; its artillery regiment may have been the 18th, but this is not confirmed. The division had only 8,000–10,000 troops and some may have been sent south as replacements. The 31st Rifle Division had been formed as the Seoul City Regiment in July and August and was redesignated a division just before the landing. It only consisted of the 31st Rifle Regiment, with much of its strength from press-ganged South Koreans.

The 105th Tank Division was in the south, but the KPA also possessed some separate tank regiments. These units were equipped with the Soviet T34/85. Armed with an 85mm gun and two machine guns, the T34 was well protected by heavy sloped armor. The 2.36in. bazooka was ineffective against it, as were 57mm and 75mm recoilless rifles and the 37mm AT guns used by the ROKA. The T34 gave the KPA a decisive edge, but large numbers were lost to UN fighter-bombers, tanks, and the 3.5in. bazooka. A KPA tank regiment was actually of battalion-size and comprised of three company-size "battalions" of ten tanks with three "companies" of three tanks. The 42d and 43d Tank Regiments in the Seoul area were apparently readying to head south.

ORDER OF BATTLE

Inch'on–Seoul Campaign

1st Marine Division (Reinforced) organization and strength

HQ Battalion, 1st MarDiv	916
1st Amphibian Tractor Battalion, FMF	868
1st Engineer Battalion	1,038
1st Medical Battalion	566
1st Motor Transport Battalion	686
7th Motor Transport Battalion, FMF	430
1st Ordnance Battalion	533
1st Shore Party Battalion[1]	648
1st Service Battalion	873
1st Signal Battalion[2]	652
1st Tank Battalion[3]	811
1st Marines	3,850
5th Marines	3,850
11th Marines (artillery) [4]	2,360
1st Combat Support Group, FMF[5]	1,291
1st Amphibian Truck Company, FMF	244
Marine Observation Squadron [6]	62
Det, Marine Tactical Air Control Squadron 2	55
Total US Marine and Navy	**19,733**
1st KMC Regiment	2,786
US Army HQ Detachment	38
US Army Signal Detachment	37
2d Engineer Special Brigade	952
73d Engineer Combat Battalion	724
96th Field Artillery Battalion (155mm Howitzer)	388
Company A, 56th Amphibious Tractor Battalion	151
50th Engineer Port Construction Company	214
65th Ordnance Ammunition Company	256
Total US Army	2,760
Grand Total	**28,039**
7th Marines (en route)[6]	5,638
Administrative Center, Pusan	182
Division Administrative Center, Kobe &	
1st Armored Amphibian Tractor Battalion[7]	1,344

1st Marine Division task organization for Inch'on Landing
HQ Battalion (+) (- detachments), 1st MarDiv
    Detachment, 163d Military Intelligence Detachment (USA)
    Detachment, 441st Counter-intelligence Corps Detachment (USA)
1st Signal Battalion (+) (- detachments)
    Detachment, 205th Signal Repair Company (USA)
    Carrier Platoon, FMF
    Detachment, 4th Signal Battalion (USA)
1st Motor Transport Battalion
1st Ordnance Battalion (- detachments)
1st Service Battalion (- detachments)
Detachment, Marine Tactical Air Control Squadron 2

BLT-3, RCT-5
3d Battalion, 5th Marines
Detachment, Company A, 1st Tank Battalion
Detachment, Air-Naval Gunfire Liaison Company, 1st Signal Battalion

Remarks:
1. Includes detachments, Naval Beach Group 1.
2. Includes Carrier Platoon, FMF.
3. Includes Tank Platoons, AT Companies, 1st and 5th Marines.
4. Includes Battery C, 1st 4.5in. Rocket Battalion, FMF.
5. Includes 1st Fumigation and Bath Platoon, 1st Aerial Delivery Platoon, and Naval Beach Group 1 (- detachments).
6. Includes attachments from divisional support battalions.
7. Includes non-deployable 17-year-olds.

Reconnaissance Detachment, 11th Marines
Team 1, Shore Party Group A

RCT-5
5th Marines (- 3d Battalion & Tank Platoon, AT Company)
Company A, 1st Engineer Battalion
Company C, 1st Medical Battalion
Detachment, Air-Naval Gunfire Liaison Company, 1st Signal Battalion
2d Battalion, 1st KMC Regiment
Company A, 1st Tank Battalion (- detachment)
Shore Party Group A (- Team 1)
Detachment, Signal Company, 1st Signal Battalion
Forward Observer & Liaison Section, 1st Battalion, 11th Marines

RCT-1
1st Marines (- Tank Platoon, AT Company)
Company A (+), 56th Amphibian Tank and Tractor Battalion (USA)
Company C (+), 1st Engineer Battalion
Company D (-), 1st Medical Battalion
Battery C, 1st 4.5in. Rocket Battalion
Detachment, Air-Naval Gunfire Liaison Company, 1st Signal Battalion
Shore Party Group B (- Team 3)
Forward Observer & Liaison Section, 2d Battalion, 11th Marines

11th Marines (- 3d Battalion)
96th Field Artillery Battalion (USA)
Detachment, Company B, 1st Engineer Battalion
1st Amphibious Truck Company, FMF

1st Tank Battalion (+) (- detachments)
Tank Platoon, AT Company, 1st Marines
Tank Platoon, AT Company, 5th Marines

1st Engineer Battalion (- detachments)

1st Shore Party Battalion (- detachments)
Shore Party Communication Section, 1st Signal Battalion
Team 3, Shore Party Group B

Reconnaissance Company, 1st MarDiv

1st Amphibian Tractor Battalion, FMF

Marine Observation Squadron 6

1st KMC Regiment (- 2d Battalion)*
* 5th Battalion, 1st KMC to join at a later date.

2d Engineer Special Brigade (+) (USA)
1st Combat Support Group (Medium), FMF (- detachments)
1st Fumigation & Bath Platoon, FMF
1st Aerial Delivery Platoon, FMF
Naval Beach Group 1 (- detachments)
7th Motor Transport Battalion, FMF
73d Engineer Combat Battalion (USA)
50th Engineer Port Construction Company (USA)
65th Ordnance Ammunition Company (USA)

RCT-7 (en route)
7th Marines
3d Battalion, 11th Marines
Company D, 1st Engineer Battalion

Company E, 1st Medical Battalion
Company D, 1st Motor Transport Battalion
Company C, 1st Shore Party Battalion
Company D, 1st Tank Battalion
Detachment, 1st Signal Battalion

7th Infantry Division organization
Division HQ & HQ Company
17th Infantry Regiment
31st Infantry Regiment
32d Infantry Regiment
17th ROK Infantry Regiment
Division Artillery
    31st Field Artillery Battalion (155mm Howitzer)
    48th Field Artillery Battalion (105mm Howitzer)
    49th Field Artillery Battalion (105mm Howitzer)
    57th Field Artillery Battalion (105mm Howitzer)
    Battery A, 15th AAA Automatic Weapons Battalion
Division Troops
    73d Tank Battalion (Medium)
    13th Engineer Combat Battalion
    7th Reconnaissance Company
Division Special Troops
    7th Medical Battalion
    7th Signal Company
    707th Ordnance Maintenance Company
    7th Quartermaster Company
    7th Military Police Company
    7th Replacement Company
    7th Counter Intelligence Corps Detachment

Korean People's Army units encountered in the Inch'on–Seoul Campaign

Only elements of many of these units were employed. They are listed in the order in which they were encountered.

Unit	Area Encountered	Estimated Strength
226th Marine Regiment	Inch'on	2,000
2d Bn (-), 918th Coast Artillery Regt	Inch'on	200
42d Tank Regiment	Between Inch'on &Seoul	500
1st Air Force Division*	Kimpo Airfield	unknown
107th Security Regiment	Kimpo area	2,500
Special Cultural Battalion	West of Yongdungp'o (re-habitation unit)	230
87th Regiment, 9th Rifle Division	Yongdungp'o	2,000
18th Rifle Division	Yongdungp'o & Seoul	8,000-10,000
25th Rifle Brigade	Seoul	4,000-5,000
43d Tank Regiment	Seoul	500
19th AA Regiment	Seoul	1,200
76th Regiment, 42d Division	Seoul	3,000
78th Independent Regiment	Seoul	2,000
513th Artillery Regiment	Seoul	1,500
10th RR Security Regiment	Seoul	900
31st Regiment, 31st Rifle Division†	Seoul	3,600
36th Bn, 111th Security Regiment	Seoul	750
75th Independent Regiment	Seoul & Uijongbu	2,000
27th Rifle Brigade	Suyuhan	5,000

* Ad hoc formation which included 107th Security Regiment and survivors of 226th Marine Regiment.

OPPOSING PLANS

THE AMERICAN PLAN – OPERATION *CHROMITE*

In the morning of June 25, 1950 Gen MacArthur flew from Tokyo into Suwon Airfield 15 miles south of Seoul. There he was met by President Syngman Rhee, the ROK minister of defense who doubled as prime minister, the US ambassador, and US advisors to the ROKA. Borrowing a car, MacArthur's entourage drove north to a point overlooking the as yet to be blown railroad bridge crossing the Han River out of Seoul. The capital was burning, artillery rounds were bursting on its north side, and the roads full of thousands of refugees. The remnants of the retreating ROK 1st, 7th, and Capital divisions were fleeing the city as the 3d and 4th NK Divisions lunged in from the north; the 6th NK Division headed for Inch'on. It was here MacArthur made the decision to turn the tide and request authority to commit ground troops and air support from President Truman. He already had a plan in mind, and it required an amphibious landing in the enemy's rear.

MacArthur is often credited as conceiving the Inch'on landing, but the true author is Donald McB. Curtis, a Pentagon staff member who prepared contingency plan SL-17 on June 19, by coincidence just days before the NK invasion. The plan presupposed an NK invasion, a retreat south, establishment of a perimeter at Pusan, and an outflanking amphibious landing to support a counteroffensive once Pusan was reinforced. MacArthur's General Headquarters (GHQ) requested copies

Here a marine 155mm M1A1 howitzer is towed by a dozer-tractor off a pontoon raft. Both marine and army divisions had one "155" battalion, and two battalions were assigned to X Corps, one being self-propelled. (USMC)

Army commanders. The 32d Infantry was the principal army unit to participate in the campaign. From left to right: Col Charles E. Beauchamp (32d Infantry), MajGen David G. Barr (7th InfDiv), MajGen Edward M. Almond (X Corps), and Marine BGen Edward A. Craig (Assistant Division Commander, 1st MarDiv). (USA)

A marine M26 Pershing heavy tank, nicknamed "Fightin' Fool," drives off an LST ramp at the base of a sea wall as the tide recedes. C-rations for a week are secured to the vehicle. (USMC)

within days of the invasion. MacArthur may not have been the author, but it was his drive and vision that saw its implementation, and of course his staff that accomplished the expanded planning to make it happen.

MacArthur's chief of staff, MajGen Edward M. Almond and his GHQ staff quickly developed an initial plan, Operation *Bluehearts*. *Bluehearts* envisioned the 24th InfDiv deploying to Pusan from Japan and driving north to Suwon to block the NK advance. It was assumed Seoul could not be held. It would be followed by the 25th InfDiv, which would position itself in the central portion of the peninsula and back up the faltering ROKA. On about July 20 an amphibious assault at Inch'on would be conducted by a hoped-for marine RCT and the 1st CavDiv to cut the NK supply line. This plan was discussed on July 4 at GHQ in Tokyo with marine representatives present. While a sound plan, it was impossible to accomplish with the available under-strength and ill-trained divisions. The NK were moving too fast and the ROKA crumbling at a proportionate rate. Of course the defeat of Task Force Smith the next day dashed any hopes of executing *Bluehearts*

Four LSTs beached at Beach Red discharge their cargo. Supply dumps can be seen to the left. Inch'on was the only US amphibious operation in which a major operational port was secured on D-Day, a factor contributing to the operation's success. (USMC)

as conceived. Still the 1st CavDiv rushed to embark, expecting the plan to be carried out. Instead, *Bluehearts* turned into an amphibious reinforcement landing at Po'hang-dong 70 miles north of Pusan. The landing was unopposed, although the NK were closing in. Po'hang was chosen as port faculties at Pusan were overly congested. While a much smaller operation, *Bluehearts* offered navy amphibious forces a much-needed shakedown before the more challenging Inch'on landing.

Even though *Bluehearts* evolved into something different, MacArthur recognized the need to cut the NK supply line and establish a force in their rear to support the Pusan breakout. It would also hurt the NK psychologically and materially as well as force them to fight on two widely separated fronts. Reestablishing Seoul as the capital only three months after the NK invasion would be a significant political victory. Inch'on was Korea's second largest port (the first being Pusan) and Kimpo Airfield was the best on the peninsula.

The Inch'on landing has been characterized as brilliant, daring, and extraordinary. It was certainly daring as the forces involved were so hastily assembled, under-trained, and lacking in rehearsal – extensive practicing and dry-runs had long been deemed essential for any amphibious operation. It was also bold because of the dangerous approach channel that was negotiated at night, the tidal hazards, and the confinement of the invasion fleet in such a small maneuver area. The doctrine of landing an amphibious force deep in the enemy's rear, especially when the friendly force dominates the sea and sky, was well established and not without precedent. The Allied landings at Anzio and Salerno, Italy in 1944, both on the west coast of a peninsula, had been equally risky for their own reasons, but successful.

MacArthur's staff continued to develop flanking landing plans. Operation Plan 100-B for Inch'on, 100-C for Kunsan on the west coast some 100 miles from Korea's southwest tip and less than halfway up the coast toward Inch'on, and 100-D at Chumunjin-up on the east coast just

The early capture of Kimpo Airfield would not only provide a base for close air support fighters, but also for resupply and medical evacuation. Here an R4C (C-47) of Marine Transport Squadron 152 offloads fuel at Kimpo. (USMC)

A marine DUKW-353 or "Duck" 2½-ton amphibious truck crawls across the Inch'on mud flats. Saplings have been laid as a corduroy road on which wire mesh matting is laid using a special rack. (USMC)

south of the 38th Parallel. Kunsan was not far enough behind the enemy's rear and the landing force could too soon meet enemy troops withdrawing from Pusan. It still left much of the NK line of communications intact. While secondary supply lines served the east coast, the Chumunjin-up course of action would not sever the main line through Seoul unless the landing force fought all the way across the peninsula. Some recommended it as they feared the hazards of the Inch'on basin, but it would have required a two-division force (with its own lengthy and vulnerable supply line) to traverse 160 miles, exposing their flanks to withdrawing enemy divisions.

For an amphibious assault of this magnitude, a 160-day planning phase was recommended; GHQ planners had 34. MacArthur issued Operation Plan 100-B for Inch'on on August 12 (D-34). He did not provide a copy to the JCS although they knew that it was underway. The National Defense Act, which outlined the relationship between the JCS and theater commanders-in-chief was nebulous, and MacArthur opted to keep things in close-hold. Two days previously the JCS had briefed President Truman that while a marine division was en route to Korea, they did not feel a landing at Inch'on was a viable course of action. FECOM pressed on with plans for the landing and the Pusan breakout.

On August 23 (D-23) a top level conference was held at FECOM headquarters in Tokyo, attended by MacArthur, Gen J. Lawton Collins (Army Chief of Staff), Adm Forrest P. Sherman (Chief of Naval Operations), ViceAdm C. Turner Joy (Naval Forces, Far East), LtGen Lemuel C. Sheperd, Jr. (Fleet Marine Force, Pacific), MajGen Edward M. Almond (FECOM Chief of Staff), MajGen Oliver P. Smith (1st MarDiv), MajGen David G. Barr (7th InfDiv), and RearAdm James H. Doyle (Attack Force Commander). The day before, MacArthur had informed MajGen Smith that his division would spearhead the Inch'on

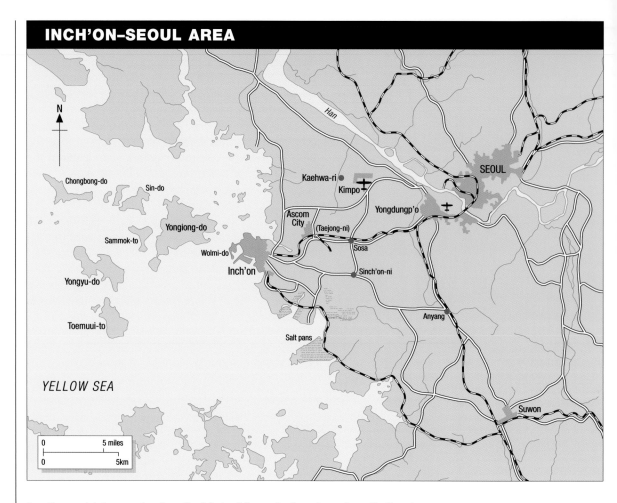

landing, which was the first Smith had heard of such a plan. Reflecting Doyle's concerns with the Inch'on tides and the treacherous channel, Smith suggested that a better landing site might be Posung-Myun just south of Inch'on. Almond dismissed this option. Oddly, neither Smith nor Sheperd were invited to the Tokyo meeting, but MajGen Barr, the follow-on division commander, was.

MacArthur was adamant that the landing would be at Inch'on. The navy's objections regarding tides, terrain, and other physical handicaps such as Wolmi-do which they feared was heavily fortified and dominated the landing beaches, were brushed aside. The navy also recommended a three- to four-day preparatory bombardment, but the FECOM staff felt such a long bombardment would eliminate tactical surprise and allow the North Koreans to shift forces to meet the landing. MacArthur felt that the recapture of Seoul would save 100,000 lives and lead to a quick end for the war, which he expected to be over by Christmas. He closed with, "We shall land at Inch'on and I shall defeat the enemy."

The navy and marines made a last effort to convince MacArthur to land at Posung-Myun, but it was dismissed. MacArthur's mind was fixed on the immediate seizure of a port to sustain the force. At the end of the meeting Doyle made the comment, "General, I have not been asked nor have I volunteered my opinion about this landing. If I were asked, however, the best I can say is Inch'on is not impossible." The navy was not the only concerned party: Gen Collins, too, held reservations regarding enemy strength and capabilities at Inch'on, which had been barely addressed. He also questioned whether Eighth Army could break out and link up on a timely basis and only received reassurances backed by no facts. MajGen Barr made a somewhat positive observation, "It's so wrong that it's right. The element of surprise will be great." Some gave it a 5,000-to-1 chance of success. MacArthur was completely confident.

Another MacArthurian blow to the marines followed when he informed LtGen Sheperd that MajGen Almond had been promised command of the as-yet-to-be-activated X Corps, the landing force. With extensive amphibious expertise, Sheperd had hoped for the command; Almond had none.

Gen Walker, commanding Eighth Army, proposed an alternative plan to Gen Collins, Army Chief of Staff. Radio intercepts indicated that the NK were going to throw every remaining unit at the perimeter in desperate hope of defeating tottering UN forces. It was known that the bulk of the forces would attack the west side of the Naktong River, mostly defended by Americans. Once the initial attacks had spent themselves Walker proposed to conduct limited objective attacks to drive the enemy to the west, as well as probing attacks by the ROKA in the north to push the NK into the mountains and away from the perimeter. A main attack would be launched northwest toward Taejon on the NK supply line and at the same time an amphibious assault conducted at Kunsan. This force, besides cutting a main coastal road and securing a secondary harbor, would attack northeast to Taejon. It was hoped that a large portion of the NK that had survived the attacks on the Naktong front would be enveloped and trapped in southwest Korea. While Collins liked the plan, MacArthur's dramatics swayed the JCS to let him have his way, although it is apparent that some thought he would choose another course of action.

On August 24 (D-22) Far East Air Force began planning the allocation of air support to both the upcoming landing and to reinforce Eighth Army's breakout. On the 26th (D-20) MacArthur announced Almond's assignment as X Corps commander upon activation of the corps in Tokyo. That same day Gen Omar N. Bradley, Chairman of the JCS, briefed President Truman on what Gen Collins and Adm Sherman had learned of the Inch'on plan at the August 23 conference. They had not been asked to approve the plan nor was MacArthur obligated to ask them to do so. While the service chiefs had reservations, Truman was optimistic. The JCS gave its conditional approval on August 28 (D-18) for a landing at Inch'on or a beach to the south, indicating they were not comfortable with the former. They required MacArthur to keep them abreast of changes and recommended that an alternative plan be developed for Kunsan.

On August 30 Commander, Naval Forces, Far East assigned Joint Task Force 7 (JTF7) to conduct the Inch'on landing. JTF7 was not activated until September 11 (D-4). The various naval task forces transporting and supporting the landing force would depart from four ports in Japan and Korea between September 5 and 13. Preliminary aerial bombardment of Wolmi-do and Inch'on would commence on September 10 (D-5) with naval shelling on the 13th (D-2).

X Corps Operation Order 1 was issued on August 28 (D-18) and received by 1st MarDiv on the 30th. The division, though, had received a

Ships of the JTF7 Transport Group take up position in the transport area outside Inch'on Harbor. (USN)

preliminary briefing on August 19 (D-27) and commenced planning. Not only was this the shortest planning time ever allotted for a divisional amphibious assault, but only a quarter of the staff was aboard the USS *Mount McKinley* (AGC-7) to undertake the myriad of planning tasks. The division issued Operation Order 2-50 on September 4 (D-11). Planning time was so short that, contrary to normal practice, the division wrote detailed landing plans for the regiments rather than the regiments and battalions preparing their own after receiving the higher echelon's order.

The X Corps operation plan had begun to be developed by the GHQ Joint Strategic Plans and Operations Group in July. It was taken over by the GHQ Special Planning Staff (aka "Force X") on August 12. This staff provided the nucleus for the X Corps staff.

The X Corps plan called for the 1st MarDiv to conduct an amphibious assault to seize Inch'on on September 15 (D-Day), secure a beachhead, advance as rapidly as possible to seize Kimpo Airfield to provide a base for close air support aircraft, and clear the south bank of the Han River. It would then assault across the Han, seize Seoul, and secure the high ground to the north. It would fortify a line to the north with reduced forces and await relief (tentatively by 3d InfDiv still in the States). The division would then recross the Han and seize a line 25 miles southeast of Seoul. The 1st MAW would provide close air support, air warning, and air control operating from Kimpo Airfield. The Pusan breakout would commence on September 16. It was considered that the NK might reinforce Inch'on–Seoul with units attacking the Perimeter. The closest were the 3d, 10th, and 13th divisions astride the Taegue-Taejon–Seoul Highway, the route the main breakout force would take.

The 7th InfDiv would land behind the marines on about D+4 and advance to secure high ground south of Seoul and the Han. It would move into Seoul, secure a line to the north to the right of the 1st MarDiv, and then conduct a reconnaissance-in-force south of Seoul where it would secure a line. Alongside the 1st MarDiv to the east, the two divisions would face south to provide the anvil to meet NK forces withdrawing before the hammer of the Eighth Army breakout.

The tides were a major planning factor. The navy wanted to make the perilous approach up the Flying Fish Channel during daylight. This meant the four-hour approach would arrive at 1130hrs and low tide. The tide would be receded by 1300hrs. The next high tide allowing landing craft to run ashore was at 1919hrs. Wolmi-do would have to be secured in the evening with only two hours of light remaining for the marines to clear the island which was honeycombed with fortifications. After the evening tide receded they would have to spend the night on an incompletely secured island at risk of infantry attacks across the exposed mud flats. The main landings into Inch'on would then be conducted during the morning high tide. This would allow the NK much of the previous day and all night to bring in reinforcements and position troops to meet the main landings.

The approach would have to be made in the pre-dawn dark and the first landing to seize Wolmi-do made during the morning high tide. The main landings into Inch'on would occur in the evening with just enough time to secure beachheads. While doctrine called for assault troops to land in amtracs, because of the 15ft seawalls, those aimed at Beach Green and Beach Red would have to land from Landing Crafts, Personnel and Vehicles (LCVPs) using scaling ladders. Amtracs would be used on Beach Blue as there was no seawall.

After a pre-landing bombardment the marine plan called for 3d Battalion, 5th Marines (3/5) to assault Wolmi-do (specifically, the 50yd-wide Beach Green on the small North Point peninsula) at 0630hrs (L-Hour), September 15. This would secure the islands dominating the harbor and the tide would soon ebb. The marines on Wolmi-do and Sowolmi-do would be on their own waiting for the evening high tide. Naval and air bombardment would continue on Inch'on and approaching NK reinforcements be forced to move in daylight.

Just prior to the landing MajGen Almond proposed three inane plans that were fortunately rejected. One was for the 8227th Army Unit (Eighth Army Raider Company), reinforced by 100 handpicked marines, to paddle 3 miles to shore in rubber boats to land 8 miles north of Inch'on, move 9 miles overland by foot to Kimpo Airfield, seize it in a surprise attack, and hold until relieved. Smith wisely refused to provide the marines, pointing out that the 5th Marines had only just withdrawn from combat and was under-strength. Furthermore, 500 17-year-olds had been pulled out of the division, there was no time for the unit and the re-assigned marines to rehearse together, and lastly, Smith needed to retain his experienced troops. It is highly unlikely the 224-man unit could have held out until relieved by the landing troops, which took three days to reach the airfield. Almond still planned to launch the raiders without the marines, but it was cancelled at the last minute. It was earlier planned to land this unit, without marines, at Kunsan far to the south to create a diversion and make it appear a division was landing, a tall order for a 124-man unit. Elements of three NK divisions in the area would have made short work of it. Another plan proposed by Almond was to land a battalion of the 32d Infantry, 7th InfDiv on Wolmi-do in the evening during the main landings, load it aboard marine trucks and tanks, and drive 20 miles to seize high ground on the edge of Seoul. Smith rejected this idea too, stating he could not afford the vehicles and felt it was a tactical impossibility. This force would also have had to be supported by air and naval gunfire; artillery on Wolmi-do was out of range. Besides tactical impracticality, all resupply would have to be by air. It took the marines eight days to reach the battalion's proposed objective. Both schemes also would have placed restrictions on fire zones forward of the advancing marines, an unnecessary hindrance.

Looking south, Inch'on burns after heavy naval and air bombardment. The white rectangular area on the waterfront beneath the black column of smoke is Beach Red where RCT-5 landed. Just to its left and hidden mostly by the smoke is Cemetery Hill. The dark area near the upper center with white smoke to its right is Observatory Hill. (USN)

The navy would control the airspace around Inch'on, with the Far East Air Force restricted from conducting operations within a 100-mile radius of Inch'on unless requested by JTF7. The air force had opposed placing such a large area under naval control, but it was approved. The navy and marines would conduct continuous air patrols in a 25-mile radius around Inch'on.

The main landings would occur at 1730hrs (H-Hour). North of Wolmi-do, the 500yd-wide Beach Red was situated on the Inch'on waterfront, but outside of the main harbor. The 5th Marines, minus 3/5, would land here and push inland up to 1,000yds to establish a 3,000-yd line, the O-A Line, stretching from a few hundred yards north of the beach and south to the east end of the Inner Tidal Basin encompassing Cemetery and Observatory hills. 1/5 would land on the left and 2/5 on the right, with both battalions coming ashore in a column of companies.

Some 4,000 yards to the southeast of Beach Red lay the 1,000-yd wide Beach Blue on the edge of Inch'on. Doctrine called for a division's two assault regiments to land adjacent to one another unless terrain restrictions or enemy dispositions dictated otherwise. In World War II the marines conducted only two landings where the landing force was separated by a considerable distance, at Tinian and Guam. The men of 2/1 would land to the left on Blue 1, and 3/1 on Blue 2 to the right; each battalion would land with two companies abreast aboard amtracs and preceded by army amphibian tanks. Blue 3 was south of and at a right angle to Blue 2 and was a questionable alternative. They would fight through an industrial area up to 3,000 yards inland to secure the 4-mile O-1 Line. The 1st Marines would control by fire the Inch'on–Seoul Highway. Key objectives were Hill 117 northeast of the beach; Hill 233, a long ridge 1,500 yards southeast of the beach; and Hill 94, a small cape flanking the beach. The plan called for 1/1 to come ashore in LCVPs 45 minutes after the assault battalions. There were no plans for RCT-5 and RCT-1 to link up on D-Day.

When Beach Red was secured, eight LSTs would beach to off-load critical ammunition and supplies before nightfall. Two artillery battalions and support troops would land on Wolmi-do at 1900hrs to provide artillery support to the marines on the mainland. The marines would maintain defensive positions through the night and commence clearing the remainder of the city, link up, and continue toward Seoul.

Intelligence

Little was known of the North Korean order of battle, dispositions, strength, and capabilities deep in the rear areas. Many units were stripped of troops to send south to Pusan. There were still substantial units in the area, although they were dispersed and under-strength.

In addition, Japanese maps and hydrographic charts were often inaccurate and outdated. Villages, streams, roads – even entire hill masses – were incorrectly positioned or omitted. Different grid systems were used, making location reporting and fire control difficult.

Detailed hydrographic data on the port of Inch'on was scarce and what was available was often suspect or conflicting. Aerial photography augmented maps, but differences in altitude and perspective complicated their use. The height of the seawalls could not be accurately determined from aerial photos. It was determined there were no manmade boat obstacles.

In an effort to collect up-to-date intelligence on the Flying Fish Channel, Wolmi-do, and Inch'on Harbor, the navy sent Lt Eugene F. Clark with two Korean interpreters by boat to Yong-hong-do island 15 miles southwest of Inch'on and on the west side of the Flying Fish Channel. Accompanied by rations, rice, and weapons, Clark established a small private "army" of teenagers from the island's friendly inhabitants and set up camp on September 1. Some of the teenagers served as coast-watchers to secure his base, the NK occupied Taebu-do 3 miles across East Channel. Others posed as fishermen to reconnoiter Wolmi-do and the harbor, reporting back to Clark with descriptions and locations of defenses, seawall and pier data, current speeds, and water depths. He captured NK sampans to obtain information from prisoners and reconnoitered the harbor himself. He even walked the low-tide mud flats proving that in some areas

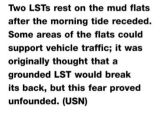

Two LSTs rest on the mud flats after the morning tide receded. Some areas of the flats could support vehicle traffic; it was originally thought that a grounded LST would break its back, but this fear proved unfounded. (USN)

Marines examine an abandoned NK trench on the outskirts of Inch'on. In the background is one of the city's industrial areas. Virtually every piece of defendable terrain inside and outside Inch'on was honeycombed with fortifications. Fortunately the NK did not possess the troops in the area to man them. (USMC)

A Soviet-supplied NK 76.2mm M1942 field gun emplaced on Wolmi-do. The wheels were intentionally removed. This extremely effective weapon served as NK divisional artillery, and was also employed as an anti-tank and coastal defense gun. Note the rice straw sandbags. (USN)

they were sufficiently firm for foot and even vehicle traffic. He also discovered that the lighthouse on Palmi-do was still operational. When Clark radioed this information he was directed to turn on the light at midnight, September 14.

A less successful reconnaissance was conducted on the night of 11–12 September by Eighth Army Raider Company. They and a smaller group of British sailors reconnoitered two beaches at Kunsan south of Inch'on. The unit was detected and taken under fire with the loss of two dead and one wounded. The reconnaissance was an effort to determine if Kunsan's beaches were suitable as alternative landing points.

In early September X Corps estimated that there were 1,500–2,500 NK troops in the Inch'on area, mostly recruits. Many of these may have been press-ganged South Koreans, a common practice. Prior to the landing the enemy estimate was revised to c.7,000 in the Inch'on–Seoul area: 1,000 in Inch'on, 5,000 in Seoul, and 500 at Kimpo. The numbers and capabilities of units that could reinforce the area after the landing were unknown, but were thought to be within a few days' march. It was assumed that some tanks would be in the area, but numbers and locations were unknown. NK air force capabilities were limited, and they possessed no jet fighters or bombers. Several models of Soviet-supplied Yakovlev and Lavochkin prop-driven fighters were in use.

THE NORTH KOREAN PLAN – TOO LITTLE TOO LATE

The formal details of the NK defense plan are unknown, so historians can only assess their actual movements and actions. It is unlikely that they possessed a well developed plan. Units available in the Inch'on–Seoul area were in constant turmoil as they passed through to the south. Other units were constantly being ordered to send replacement drafts south. There was also no single known major command in control of the area other than possibly some regional administrative headquarters. Such a headquarters would not have been suited for the planning, command, and control of defensive and counterattack operations. Part of the plan may have been to use whatever units were available, to include rear service troops, as ad hoc defense forces. Elements of the 18th and 19th KPA Divisions were known to be in Seoul. The NK probably felt there was little chance of a major amphibious landing directly into Inch'on because of the very reasons that made the JCS, navy, and others hesitant.

Little was known of NK defensive techniques as UN forces had only experienced their offensive tactics. Naval forces were experienced with NK coast artillery: 76mm, 85mm, and 122mm. These Soviet-made guns (mostly 76mm at Inch'on) were often emplaced in open positions. There were scores of prepared artillery, mortar positions, and trenches throughout Inch'on, but most were unoccupied. Over a hundred hardened positions were detected by aerial reconnaissance. It was assessed that the NK had only minimal troops in the area to defend against amphibious raiders. Because of the many prepared, but unoccupied fortifications, the NK probably planned to rush troops to the city from Seoul if a major landing looked imminent. This was another good reason for US forces to establish beachheads within Inch'on on D-Day itself. Delaying the establishment of beachheads would have given the enemy the cover of darkness to move up reinforcements. There were no air defenses.

The marines established their beachheads and cleared Inch'on reasonably easily. Resistance was uneven in the intervening towns on the road to Seoul, Ascom City, Sosa, Kimpo, and Yongdungp'o. Counterattacks were piecemeal, usually small in strength and unsupported by artillery. While the original NK plan may have envisioned a defense on the Han River, resistance there was light. The NK establlished their defense line in the hills on the west and northwest sides of Seoul. Strongpoints were built within the city, and streets were barricaded, but there were no identifiable defense lines within Seoul.

OPERATION *CHROMITE*

PRELIMINARIES AND THE APPROACH

The 1st MarDiv, with the 1st Prov MarBde but minus RCT-5 and the en route RCT-7, assembled at Kobe, Japan between August 29 and September 3. With the division billeted ashore and aboard transports, supplies and equipment were transferred from cargo ships to assault ships. On the 3rd, Typhoon Jane slammed into Kobe suspending loading operations for 24 hours. Only the assault elements could be combat-loaded. Some 2,750 army troops of artillery, tank, and engineer units were attached. The complaints of parents to congressmen regarding the dispatch of 17-year-olds into combat forced the Secretary of the Navy to order 500 young men to be pulled from units. They were re-assigned to the 1st Armored Amphibian Tractor Battalion, which was to remain in Kobe. It was expected that this unit would be under-employed and had been gutted by transferring many of its troops to the 1st Tank Battalion. The 17-year-olds would be sent as combat replacements as they turned 18. Tanks and amtracs had to be serviced, and water had damaged tank ammunition and replacement clothing. A joint shore party organization was thrown together under the army's 2d Engineer Special Brigade. There was a great deal of confusion during the cross-loading and embarkation. As there was no time for detailed load planning, much less exercises and rehearsals, only the extent of the veteran marines' amphibious experiences ensured a successful

LST-859, its forecastle festooned with 40mm and 20mm guns, and its weather deck crowded with vehicles, beaches on the Beach Red seawall. Eight LSTs beached here by 1900hrs on D-Day to off-load critical supplies and equipment. Beside the LST is an LCM. In the foreground, marines take cover in captured trenches. The Nippon Flour Company burns in the background. (USMC)

LCVPs move the line of departure in column. They will form into a line before making their run to Beach Green on Wolmi-do. In the background Inch'on burns. (USMC)

embarkation. Most of the amtrac crews had not driven their vehicles in the water. The combat-exhausted marines of RCT-5 at Pusan rushed to load and prepared to lead an amphibious assault. When the brigade merged back into the division on September 13 the brigade commander became the assistant division commander and the staffs combined.

Gen Walker, commanding the hard-pressed Eighth Army, wanted to hold back the 1st Prov MarBde from Inch'on. It was a reasonable request, but Gen Smith was counting on RCT-5 to conduct the critical Wolmi-do and Beach Red assaults. Smith was charged with conducting a complex amphibious assault using units lacking either amphibious training or rehearsals. At least RCT-5 was blooded and, as a result of their combat experience, knew how to operate together smoothly. A conference was held on September 3 to address the issue. Almond asked Smith if RCT-7 would arrive in time to be substituted. Receiving a negative answer, he proposed that the 7th InfDiv's 32d Infantry be employed. Smith responded that virtually none of the leaders of the 32d had any amphibious experience. If the 32d was substituted for the 5th, the scheme of maneuver would have to be drastically changed. RCT-1 would have to be given the 5th's mission of landing on Wolmi-do, the Beach Blue landing would be canceled, there would be a delay securing a beachhead in southern Inch'on and the highway would be blocked as the inexperienced 32d would have to follow the 1st ashore on Red: all in all, an unacceptable risk.

Adm Struble suggested the alternative of withdrawing the brigade from Pusan as planned and positioning a 7th InfDiv RCT offshore as a floating reserve. Once the breakout occurred this RCT would be released to follow the division into Inch'on. This is the course of action that was finally followed.

The 17th ROK Infantry Regiment was to be attached to RCT-5, but the 17th might not be able to be released from its positions on the Pusan perimeter. The 1st Prov MarBde chief of staff proposed the 1st KMC Regiment be substituted and GHQ approved this.

The division had 29,731 marines, soldiers, and sailors assigned for the assault. They were loaded aboard an amphibious command ship, six assault transports, eight assault cargo transports, three destroyer-transports,

An LCVP carrying 3d Platoon, Company H, 2d Battalion, 5th Marines makes its run for Wolmi-do. Note the wooden scaling ladders built in Japan. (USMC)

3d Platoon, A/5 Marines storm ashore on Wolmi-do over the seawall using scaling ladders. (See Battlescene 1, page 66 for details.)

three LSDs, 49 LSTs, one LSM, and 12 LSUs. TF90, the attack force, departed for Inch'on on different dates to ensure secrecy, accommodate the different ships' speeds, and to rendezvous in the South China Sea southwest of Korea. Divided into movement groups, the Pontoon Movement Group departed Yokohama on September 5, the LSM(R) Group from Yokohama on the 9th, Tractor Groups A and B left Kobe on the 10th, Transport Group from Kobe on the 11th, and the Advance Attack Group left Pusan on the 13th. The 1st Prov MarBde was disengaged from the Pusan perimeter at midnight on September 5. The third rifle companies and replacements for the battalion arrived by air from Japan. The 1st MAW headquarters departed Kobe aboard ship as Tactical Air Command, X Corps under BGen Thomas J. Cushman, the assistant 1st MAW commander.

Even the departure was a gamble, as Typhoon Kezia, much stronger than the earlier Typhoon Jane, was bearing down on the East China Sea, but fortunately it curved more to the north, although the fleet felt its effects. The fleet entered the now quiet Yellow Sea screened by the blockade and screening Force and headed north.

The 1st MarDiv's final operation plan was briefed to Almond on the 6th when he was inspecting the division at Kobe. He had previously inspected the 7th InfDiv August 31–September 3. Almond approved the plan, but felt the marines' movements ashore were too slow. He urged quickly securing Kimpo Airfield and moving on to Seoul. Almond was briefed on the 7th InfDiv's plans on the 9th. He was concerned about co-ordination and liaison with the marines, which would prove difficult. The marine units were briefed on the operation's objective and plans while en route.

The preliminary bombardment commenced on September 10 (D-5) when three flights of marine Corsairs from the USS *Badoeng Strait* (CVE-116) and *Sicily* (CVE-118) saturated Wolmi-do with napalm to burn off trees and reveal defenses. Naval carrier planes pounded Inch'on and Seoul on the 12th and 13th. On the 10th a ROK patrol boat discovered the NK laying mines in the channel. Floating mines were discovered in Flying Fish Channel on the morning of the 13th (D-2) as destroyers and cruisers moved in to soften the objective. The ships pounded Wolmi-do and Inch'on as navy and marine planes bombed enemy positions. NK coastal guns returned fire and most were destroyed after revealing themselves. Three destroyers were hit, but damage was minimal. More mines were discovered as the ships departed, but were destroyed and no more were encountered. At midnight on the 14th, naval Lt Eugene Clark switched on the lighthouse on Inch'on's channel. Three hours later the Advance Attack Group steamed past, led by the USS *Mansfield* (DD-728). At 0454hrs navy and marine fighter-bombers began orbiting Inch'on. Four cruisers and seven destroyers anchored in a line along the channel and opened fire on the island at 0545hrs with 5-, 6-, and 8-in. guns. At 0600hrs Corsairs made their first run on Wolmi-do, blasting it with bombs and rockets. The air attacks ceased at 0615hrs, three LSM(R)s closed in and launched hundreds of 4.5-in. rockets.

ASSAULT: D-DAY

Aboard the USS *Mount McKinley* L-Hour was confirmed at 0630hrs. The marines of 3/5 were boated aboard their LCVPs by 0600hrs and on signal made their run to Beach Green on the short peninsula jutting from the north end of Wolmi-do. The first wave of seven LCVPs hit the beach at 0633hrs. The underwater demolition team had failed to clear boat wreckage from the beach, and landing craft had to maneuver about. Company H, reinforced by a Company G platoon, stormed ashore as fighters strafed 50 yards in front of the marines. The second wave brought in the remainder of the two companies two minutes later. Only random shots greeted the marines. Pausing briefly to re-organize, Company G, 3d Battalion, 5th Marines (G/5), turned south and drove up Radio Hill, meeting light resistance and stunned, surrendering defenders. The American flag was hoisted atop the hill at 0655hrs.

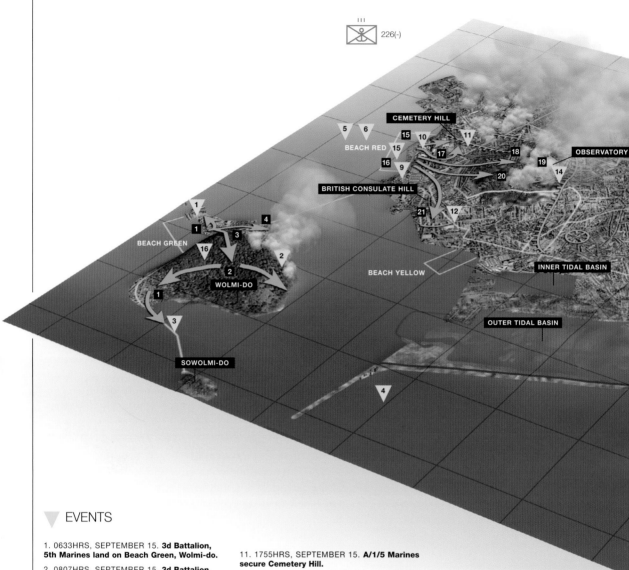

226(-)

CEMETERY HILL

5 6
BEACH RED 15
15 10
11
15
17 18
16 9 OBSERVATORY
19
20 14
BRITISH CONSULATE HILL

BEACH GREEN
1
1
16 3 4
2
2 21 12
WOLMI-DO
BEACH YELLOW
1
INNER TIDAL BASIN
3
SOWOLMI-DO OUTER TIDAL BASIN

4

▼ EVENTS

1. 0633HRS, SEPTEMBER 15. **3d Battalion, 5th Marines land on Beach Green, Wolmi-do.**

2. 0807HRS, SEPTEMBER 15. **3d Battalion, 5th Marines secure Wolmi-do.**

3. 1200HRS, SEPTEMBER 15. **3d Battalion, 5th Marines complete mop-up of Wolmi-do and Sowolmi-do.**

4. 1300HRS, SEPTEMBER 15. **Morning tide completely receded.**

5. 1705HRS, SEPTEMBER 15. **Three LSM(R)s launch 6,000 rockets in vicinity of Beaches Blue and Red.**

6. 1724HRS, SEPTEMBER 15. **Beaches Blue and Red assault waves cross line of departure.**

7. 1730HRS, SEPTEMBER 15. **3d Battalion, 1st Marines land on Beach Blue 1.**

8. 1730HRS, SEPTEMBER 15. **2d Battalion, 1st Marines land on Beach Blue 2.**

9. 1731HRS, SEPTEMBER 15. **2d Battalion, 5th Marines land on Beach Red.**

10. 1733HRS, SEPTEMBER 15. **1st Battalion, 5th Marines land on Beach Red.**

11. 1755HRS, SEPTEMBER 15. **A/1/5 Marines secure Cemetery Hill.**

12. 1800HRS, SEPTEMBER 15. **E/2/5 Marines secure British Consulate Hill.**

13. 1830HRS, SEPTEMBER 15. **1st Battalion, 1st Marines (Regimental Reserve) begin landing on Beach Blue.**

14. 1845HRS, SEPTEMBER 15. **C/1/5 Marines secure Observatory Hill.**

15. 1900HRS, SEPTEMBER 15. **Eight resupply LSTs beach at Beach Red.**

16. 1900HRS, SEPTEMBER 15. **1st & 2d Battalions (105mm), 11th Marines land on Wolmi-do and ready to deliver supporting fires at 2150hrs.**

17. 1919HRS, SEPTEMBER 15. **Evening tide reaches full height (evening twilight 1909hrs).**

18. 2230HRS, SEPTEMBER 15. **F/2/1 Marines secure Hill 117 to cover Inch'on–Seoul Highway with fire.**

D-DAY, INCH'ON, SEPTEMBER 15, 1950

1st MarDiv launched their amphibious assault to seize Inch'on on September 15 (D-Day), they quickly secured the beachheads and advanced as rapidly as possible on September 16 to secure Hill 117, nearing their ultimate objective of seizing Kimpo Airfield to provide a base for close air support aircraft, and clear the south bank of the Han River.

Note: Gridlines are shown at intervals of 500 meters

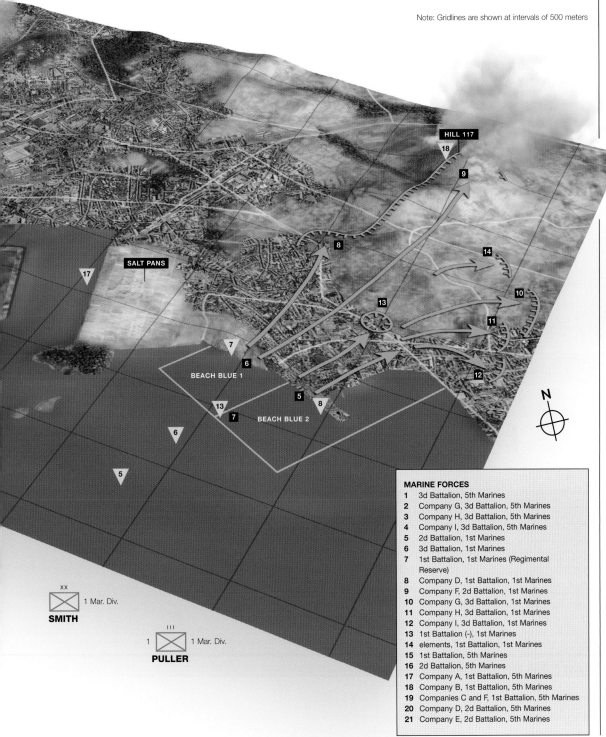

MARINE FORCES

1	3d Battalion, 5th Marines
2	Company G, 3d Battalion, 5th Marines
3	Company H, 3d Battalion, 5th Marines
4	Company I, 3d Battalion, 5th Marines
5	2d Battalion, 1st Marines
6	3d Battalion, 1st Marines
7	1st Battalion, 1st Marines (Regimental Reserve)
8	Company D, 1st Battalion, 1st Marines
9	Company F, 2d Battalion, 1st Marines
10	Company G, 3d Battalion, 1st Marines
11	Company H, 3d Battalion, 1st Marines
12	Company I, 3d Battalion, 1st Marines
13	1st Battalion (-), 1st Marines
14	elements, 1st Battalion, 1st Marines
15	1st Battalion, 5th Marines
16	2d Battalion, 5th Marines
17	Company A, 1st Battalion, 5th Marines
18	Company B, 1st Battalion, 5th Marines
19	Companies C and F, 1st Battalion, 5th Marines
20	Company D, 2d Battalion, 5th Marines
21	Company E, 2d Battalion, 5th Marines

MacArthur aboard the *Mount McKinley* simply said, "That's it. Let's get a cup of coffee." H/5 cleared the North Point and the industrial area, as well as the causeway access to Inch'on. I/5 followed behind H/5 and was surprised to find a bypassed NK platoon making hit-and-duck grenade attacks. The marine tank platoon accompanying 3/5 sealed them in their holes with a dozer tank. Some 30 North Koreans surrendered after two 90mm tank rounds were fired into a tunnel. Mop-up continued as marines swept over the island. Engineers laid AT mines on the causeway and H/5 established a roadblock, covered by tanks from 1st Tank Battalion's Company A. At 0800hrs the marines radioed to the flagship that Wolmi-do was secure. The much-feared island dominating the harbor was in marine hands. MacArthur announced, "The Navy and Marines have never shone more brightly than this morning."

A G/5 infantry/tank team advanced down the south causeway to Sowolmi-do at 1000hrs. An NK platoon pinned them down and the islet was saturated with napalm by marine fighters and barraged with mortars. The islet was secured at 1115hrs. As I/5 dug in on North Point, and H/5 in the industrial area, G/5 on Radio Hill and Sowolmi-do prepared for possible attacks across the mud flats from Inch'on. Mutually supporting trenches covered the island, along with gun positions. Mop-up was completed at noon. A very small number of NKs escaped by swimming to Inch'on, but 108 dead were counted and 136 prisoners taken. There were estimates of 150 more dead buried in the island's collapsed positions and tunnels. Marine casualties were 17 wounded.

The tide receded by 1300hrs. No NK tanks charged down the causeway, no infantry swarmed across the mud flats. Only a few civilians were spotted in Inch'on streets. The 3/5 observation post on Radio Hill called in a couple of fire missions and reported the locations of gun emplacements. The accompanying shore party group unloaded ammunition and supplies from beached LSUs that had followed the assault waves, and a reconnaissance party selected positions for the two artillery battalions that would arrive in the evening. Because of the almost complete lack of enemy activity in Inch'on, the 3/5 commander requested permission to send an infantry tank force into the city to reconnoiter or secure Beach Red. Caution prompted the commander to deny this permission. The high tide began flooding at 1400hrs at a rate of 3-½ knots, faster than expected. H-Hour was confirmed as 1730hrs. Marine Corsairs and navy Skyraiders began to hit targets in Inch'on, coordinated with naval gunfire commencing at H-180 minutes. Rain squalls drifted through the area and Beach Blue was covered by overcast and smoke. Assault troops soon began boating aboard almost 200 LCVPs, 70 LCMs, 12 LSUs, 164 amtracs, and 85 DUKW amphibious trucks. Destroyer-transports took up station off of Beaches Red and Blue and a patrol boat off Green to guide in the artillery and cargo landing craft.

At 1645hrs the 18 army amphibious tanks crossed the line of departure heading for Beach Blue, with RCT-1 following aboard amtracs. In the transport area 5 miles to the south the LCVPs headed for Red and Green. The gun ships began blasting Inch'on and the LSM(R)s launched 6,000 rockets into the city in 20 minutes. The marines in the pitching Higgins boats and amtracs riding in under gloomy skies and roaring gunfire, drenched in rain and spray, knew they were assaulting directly into a large Asian city, something that had never been attempted.

BEACH RED, 1730–1830HRS

At H-8 minutes RCT-5 (-3/5) crossed the line of departure in their LCVPs heading for Beach Red to the northeast of Wolmi-do. On Wolmi-do 3/5 opened a covering fire of machine guns and mortars backed by tanks. An engineer team advanced down the causeway to clear a route for the tanks that would meet the Beach Red troops. Marine fighters streaked down, strafing the seawall behind LSM(R) barrages. The approaching LCVPs, riding the still-flooding tide, encountered only light fire. At 1733hrs A/5 landed on the left and the assault platoons gained the seawall with little difficulty using scaling ladders. They advanced toward Cemetery Hill. At 1731hrs E/5 landed on the right and made for British Consulate Hill. They met little resistance, but A/5 lost several men to submachine-gun fire and the rest were pinned down in a trench behind the seawall. A machine-gun bunker was silenced with grenades. The second wave was late, but A/5's 2d Platoon pressed on unopposed to secure the Asahi Brewery. Part of A/5 was pinned down, however, when the second wave landed on the beach. 1stLt Baldomero Lopez was killed attempting to knock out a pillbox, which also killed a flamethrower team.

With 1st Platoon pinned, the 2d Platoon charged up Cemetery Hill flushing out and capturing NKs. On the crest, scores of NK soldiers emerged from trenches to the platoon's dismay, but only to surrender. This was the 226th Marine Regiment's mortar company dazed by the heavy bombardment. Cemetery Hill, which dominated Beach Red had been taken in ten minutes without a casualty on its slopes. On the right, E/5 moved inland gaining the railroad and then the Nippon Flour Company building to the south. Here they re-organized and moved on unopposed to British Consulate Hill, which they secured at 1845hrs. Twenty-two landing waves would follow. The following C/5 was tasked with seizing the north half of Observatory Hill and D/5 the south half. There was confusion on the beach as waves of men were arriving so fast that units were intermingling.

At 1830hrs the eight LSTs bound for Beach Red crossed the line of departure. Seeing the congestion of marines on the beach they assumed they were not able to fight their way inland. NKs on Observatory Hill opened fire with machine guns and mortars hitting some LSTs. The LSTs returned fire with 40mm and 20mm guns, but they also fired on positions held by marines, driving them off Cemetery Hill and killing one and wounding 23 in the Nippon Flour Company. Some marines directed fire on the LSTs until they received the message to cease fire. All eight LSTs were berthed by 1900hrs and there was a rush to off load them before the next high tide, and the arrival of more ships. A C/5 platoon reached the saddle between the two main peaks on Observatory Hill at 1845hrs. With a non-operational radio, they were unable to notify anyone of their success. Because of the "missing" platoon whose position was unknown, and delays on the beach, B/5 was ordered to take over C/5's mission, and with D/5 prepared to attack the hill. At 2000hrs B/5 reached the top with only six wounded. For some reason D/5 thought part of E/5 was already on southern Observatory Hill. They simply marched to the hilltop up a street, but rather than meeting E/5, they ran into NK defenders. A short firefight developed, with the company losing one dead and three wounded. The NK were driven off as darkness

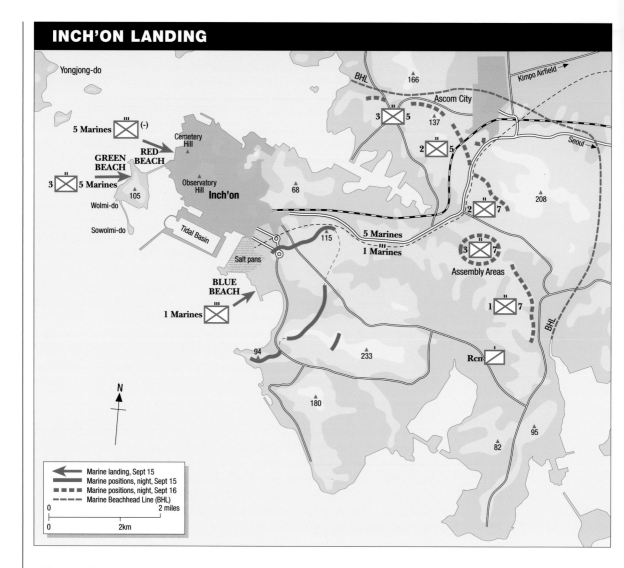

Yongjong-do
BHL
△166
Kimpo Airfield →
Ascom City
3 ⊠ 5
137
5 Marines ⊠ (-)
2 ⊠ 5
Cemetery Hill
RED BEACH
Seoul →
GREEN BEACH
3 ⊠ 5 Marines
105
Observatory Hill
Inch'on
△68
△208
Wolmi-do
2 ⊠ 7
Sowolmi-do
Tidal Basin
△115
5 Marines
1 Marines
3 ⊠ 7
Salt pans
Assembly Areas
BLUE BEACH
1 ⊠ 7
1 Marines ⊠
BHL
△94
△233
Rcn ⊠
N

Marine landing, Sept 15
Marine positions, night, Sept 15
Marine positions, night, Sept 16
Marine Beachhead Line (BHL)
0   2 miles
0   2km

△180
△95
△82

fell. An F/5 platoon was placed in a gap in the line and Observatory Hill was secured. All units had reached the O-A Line, but there was a gap to the south of Observatory Hill and the Inner Tidal Basin. This was outposted by F/5 troops and the remainder of the company established a position beside the basin after midnight.

Beach Blue was to the southeast of the Outer Tidal Basin and salt pans. RCT-1 was loaded aboard LSTs, along with the amtracs that would run them ashore. The rain, haze, smoke, and brisk current, coupled with inexperienced amtrac crews and no compasses in the amtracs led to some confusion. Only a few mortar rounds were received as the first waves ran for shore. The army amphibian tanks advanced inland but were halted by an earth slide. At 1730hrs the 3/1 assault amtracs came ashore on Blue 1. On the left, D/1 remained mounted, moved inland until halted by the earth slide, and dismounted to continue on. On the right, F/1 dismounted, cleared a knoll, and moved inland, but some of the company's amtracs had grounded on mud flats. On Blue 2 the 3/1 landing was made at 1740hrs because of problems at the line of departure and amtracs were scattered in the smoke and haze.

Insufficient guide boats were available and the amtracs could not always find the boat lanes. G/1 landed on the left and I/1 on the right with amtracs intermingled between waves. Some landed on Blue 3 to the right. A drainage ditch, the boundary between 2/1 and 3/1, blocked some of the amtracs. The assault troops were held up briefly and moved inland through dense smoke and burning buildings that obscured landmarks. Despite the confusion, few casualties were suffered. After the third wave, the following amtracs became seriously scattered and the companies required additional time to assemble as it grew darker. The regimental reserve, 1/1, was to land aboard LCVPs at 1845hrs, but was misdirected and scattered with some boats landing at the Outer Tidal Basin before relaunching. Regardless, the battalion assembled a half-mile inland, but an hour late.

D/1 secured its road intersection at 2000hrs and F/1 occupied most of Hill 117 to cover the Inch'on–Seoul Highway. At 1900hrs I/1 seized part of Hill 223 and G/1 reached its blocking position at 1930hrs. Most of G/1 filled the gap between I/1 and G/1, while one of its platoons seized Hill 94 on a cape south of the beaches. Thirty enemy dead were found on the well-entrenched objective. RCT-1 had successfully occupied its O-1 Line. An H/1 platoon was to have secured Hill 233 2,000yd to the west, but the darkness and rough terrain allowed the platoon to reach only Hill 180 at half the distance. Having crossed the causeway into Incho'on, 3/5 linked up with the rest of the regiment at 2000hrs as the reserve. Both regiments settled down for a long, rainy, but quiet night. D-Day casualties were 21 dead, one missing, 174 wounded, and 14 non-battle injuries; a far cry from the dire predictions of many of the commanders.

In the evening on Wolmi-do DUKW amphibian trucks landed 1/11 and 2/11 Marines' 105mm howitzers to support RCT-5 and RCT-1, respectively. In addition, 4/11 landed on Beach Red in support of RCT-5 on D+1, and they were followed by the 96th Field Artillery Battalion on D+2 to support RCT-1; both were armed with 155mm artillery.

Some 500 tons of supplies and equipment were off loaded from each of the eight LSTs beached on Red so they could retract at the morning tide. Resupply of the assault units went as planned and the shore party accomplished many successes such as restoring trains into operation at the Inch'on railyard. In three days trains were hauling troops and supplies to Ascom City.

Based on the necessity of getting out of Inch'on as soon as possible, the order to continue the attack after dawn was issued that night. RCT-5 would push inland to the O-2 Line placing it abreast RCT-1's O-1 Line to form a continuous boundary. The 1st Korean Marine Corps Regiment (henceforth 1 KMC) would land at dawn and mop-up the city. D+1 was clear and mild when the attack began at 0600hrs with RCT-5 advancing in column: 2/5, 1/5, and 3/5. The city was deserted and eerie as the troops moved out. Two hills on the north side of the highway were occupied by 2/5, who continued to advance beyond the O-2 Line to link-up with 2/1 at Hill 117 at 0900hrs. Marine fighters discovered six T34 tanks in Kangsong-ni 5 miles ahead of the marines and destroyed them. To the south, 1/1 became the regimental reserve as 3/1 swept the Munhang Peninsula to the south. Resistance was negligible in all zones, although numerous prisoners were taken, heavy weapons captured, and

Troops of Company H, 3d Battalion, 5th Marines man a roadblock on the causeway connecting Wolmi-do to mainland Inch'on. They are armed with a 3.5in. M20 bazooka and a .30cal M1919A4 light machine gun. The black tubes are for bazooka rockets. (USMC)

the area was found to be well fortified. The NK lacked the forces to conduct a counterattack as the marines broadened their foothold. The advance was rushed rapidly to the O-3 Line, a 3-mile-long line at the base of the conjoined Inch'on and Munhang peninsulas, 1 to $1\frac{1}{2}$ miles beyond the O-2 Line.

At 1045hrs the order was given to advance toward the Force Beachhead Line (FBHL), a right-angle line anchored on the sea at both ends. The 5-mile-long north side ran parallel with the Inch'on–Seoul Highway, then turned south on a 7-mile front. It encompassed the southern half of Ascom City and the Namdong Peninsula to the south. The highway was the boundary between the two regiments. The attack was launched at 1335hrs. When the 5th Marines reached Kansong-ni they found three of the T34s still operational, but they were destroyed by marine tanks before they could fire. One of the six had escaped. The 5th Marines dug in on a line of hills along the north side of the FBHL and stretching southeast outside of Ascom and 3,000 yards short of the FBHL. The 1st Marines took up night positions south of the highway and farther south on the Namdong Peninsula. Only sniping had been encountered during the day, costing the division four dead and 21 wounded. Some 120 NKs were killed and 30 prisoners taken. The division command post was established on the southeast outskirts of Inch'on by noon. The amphibious assault phase was completed 24 hours after the landing.

THE DRIVE TO KIMPO: D+1 TO D+2

The night of September 16–17 was quiet. The reality was that the NK in Seoul did not know marine locations and believed they were still in Inch'on. That night D/5 occupied a hill on the west side of the Inch'on–Seoul Highway and outposted a knoll 200 yards to the northeast covering a bend in the road on the edge of Ascom City. These positions were reinforced by F/1 to the south and a platoon of tanks with bazookas and recoilless rifles covering the road. A column of six T34s and 200 infantrymen approached just before dawn. As the unsuspecting NKs passed the outpost they were engaged and wiped out in short order. MacArthur visited the battlefield that day.

The next move was to seize the critical Kimpo Airfield 6 miles to the northeast of Ascom City. At 0700hrs the attack began, with 2/5 moving up the Inch'on–Seoul Highway, and then swinging north into Ascom City, two square miles of homes, factories, and storage facilities which was occupied by NK survivors from Inch'on. 3/1 KMC attacked through 2/5 into the west side of Ascom. The 2d Engineer Special Brigade relieved the rest of 1 KMC of Inch'on security later in the day. At 0900hrs 2/5 began fighting its way up the east side of the complex. Men of 3/5 moved into the west side to support 3/1 KMC, which moved north to occupy hills west of Kimpo. Supported by tanks, 2/5 followed roads leading out of Ascom to the northeast toward Kimpo, while 1/5 took up positions to the south of Kimpo. Outside Ascom, no enemy was to be found and the road was clear to Kimpo. Meanwhile, 2/5 advanced north to the airfield and at 1800hrs D/5 was on the south end of the runway experiencing little opposition.

The airfield was surrounded by villages and base facilities and proved difficult to clear, even without resistance. There was an afternoon skirmish around the train station, as well as sniping as the marines closed in on their night positions. The division was advised that RCT-7 had arrived at Kobe, was preparing to re-embark, and would arrive at Inch'on on the 21st.

The NK 1st Air Force Division, a hodge-podge of service and combat units including survivors of Inch'on, was attempting to establish a defense, but was sitting on unfavorable terrain between Kimpo and the Han River. They were disorganized and panicked at the speed of the American attack; many deserted. Regardless, three counterattacks were launched at 2/5 during the night, but only a few hundred men were committed without supporting fire, the first at 0300hrs. One outpost

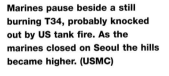

Marines pause beside a still burning T34, probably knocked out by US tank fire. As the marines closed on Seoul the hills became higher. (USMC)

BEACH RED SEAWALL, 1733HRS, SEPTEMBER 15
(pages 66–67)

The first wave to land on Beach Red was made up of four landing craft, vehicle and personnel (LCVP) (1) carrying A/5 Marines assault platoons on the left tasked with seizing Cemetery Hill. In addition four LCVPs with two assault platoons from E/5 were charged with securing British Consulate Hill on the right flank. From Wolmi-do 1,000yd to the southwest 3/5, who had landed earlier, provided covering fire. LCVPs were employed because the seawall could not be negotiated by amtracs. It was felt LCVPs could clear the area more quickly than amtracs had they been used to nose up to the seawall and disembark troops. Room had to be made for eight follow-on landing ships, tank (LST) carrying ammunition and supplies. Each LCVP was equipped with two makeshift scaling ladders (2). Platoons were split between two LCVPs to form boat teams of 20-plus men. The boat team concept was implemented in World War II. Each boat team, under an officer or NCO, was task-organized and augmented with machine guns, 3.5in. bazookas, and flamethrowers from the company weapons platoon and battalion assault platoon. They would fight inland as boat teams until the situation stabilized and they reconstituted into squads and platoons. 1stLt Baldomero Lopez's (3) 3d Platoon, A/5 came ashore in the second wave. The platoon was pinned down by machine-gun fire from behind-the-beach pillboxes and casualties mounted. 1stLt Lopez attempted to attack one pillbox (4) with a grenade and was hit, but sacrificed his life to protect his exposed men. His

Medal of Honor citation best describes this Naval Academy graduate's sacrifice:
"For conspicuous gallantry and intrepidity at the risk of his life above and beyond the call of duty as a Rifle Platoon Commander of Company A, First Battalion, Fifth Marines, First Marine Division (Reinforced), in action against enemy aggressor forces during the Inch'on invasion in Korea on 15 September 1950. With his platoon First Lieutenant Lopez was engaged in the reduction of immediate enemy beach defenses after landing with the assault waves. Exposing himself to enemy fire, he moved forward alongside a bunker and prepared to throw a hand grenade into the next pillbox whose fire was pinning down that sector of the beach. Taken under fire by an enemy automatic weapon and hit in the right shoulder and chest as he lifted his arm to throw, he fell backward and dropped the deadly missile. After a moment, he turned and dragged his body forward in an effort to retrieve the grenade and throw it. In critical condition from pain and loss of blood, and unable to grasp the grenade firmly enough to hurl it, he chose to sacrifice himself rather than endanger the lives of his men and, with a sweeping motion of his wounded arm, cradled the grenade under him and absorbed the full impact of the explosion."
His platoon's two flamethrower operators (5) were hit attempting to destroy the bunker. The 2d Platoon on the right, as yet to suffer any losses, were directed to support the 3d and they were able to clear the bunkers as 1st Platoon assaulted Cemetery Hill to allow follow-on waves to land safely. Only two other Medals of Honor were awarded at Inch'on, one of which was posthumous.

marine platoon was forced to withdraw back to its company when a T34 appeared, as the platoon lacked anti-tank weapons. The second attack was at 0500hrs, and the last at dawn was disrupted by 1/5. The area around the airfield was cleared by 1000hrs on the 18th and high ground to the east soon secured. Marine casualties were light, while the NK lost over 100 dead and ten prisoners. On September 19 Tactical Air Command, X Corps was established on Kimpo and three fighter squadrons flew in from Japan to commence operations.

On the morning of the 17th, RCT-1 was hit by a company attack in its positions to the south of Ascom, but it was dispersed by F/1. The lead battalions moved out to attack eastward south of RCT-5. They were soon enmeshed in firefights in the hills, with E/1 pinned down. The attack continued, but a surprise assault pushed back part of 3/1. A counter-attack was launched and the area cleared. Marine losses were light and the NK lost 250 men and 70 prisoners, as well as a T34 and six AT guns destroyed. Almost 5,000 yards had been gained and new positions were assumed on a line stretching from the Ascom–Sosa Highway south with 2/1, 3/1, and 1/1 on line. The division reconnaissance company patrolled the Namdong Peninsula to the south.

In the meantime, Eighth Army broke out of the Pusan perimeter on the 16th. It took three days of hard fighting to secure a bridgehead on the far side of the Naktong and commence the drive to Seoul. On the same day, the 19th, the 1st MarDiv CP moved into Oeoso-ri 1–1½ miles southeast of Kimpo. The 7th InfDiv began landing at Inch'on on the 18th with the 32d Infantry the first to come ashore, accompanied by the 49th Field Artillery Battalion. The 3d InfDiv, sailing from the States, would not arrive in time to participate in the campaign, but the 187th ARCT would arrive on the 23rd.

CROSSING THE HAN RIVER

The morning of the 18th found RCT-5 on the move northeast of Kimpo. There was insignificant resistance and once its objectives were occupied the battalions conducted patrols to the front: 1/1 and 3/1 KMC secured the base of the Kimpo Peninsula on the RCT-5's left flank. The 17th ROK Regiment landed at Inch'on on the 18th and was attached to the 1st MarDiv to patrol the area between Ascom and the sea where scattered NK were holding out. On the morning of the 18th RCT-1 attacked east focusing on Sosa and Hill 123 behind the town in the northern portion of its zone. Naval gunfire softened up what were thought to be strong enemy positions. The assault was led by 2/1, then 3/1 passed through aboard amtracs and Ducks. By noon they were in Sosa experiencing very light opposition; 3/1 then occupied Hill 123. On the left 1/1 advanced 4,000 yards. Both regiments dug in for the night.

On the same day reports from air observers and civilians from across the division's front indicated the NK were concentrating west of Yongdungp'o and north of the Han. The enemy east of Kimpo was withdrawing toward Yongdungp'o and concentrations were spotted on the Kimpo Peninsula to the northwest. Other troops were moving into Seoul from the north and east. It was apparent the marines were going to be hit with multiple frontal and flanking attacks. In the afternoon

TANK AMBUSH AT ASCOM CITY, SEPTEMBER 17
(pages 70–71)

On the night of September 16 the 5th Marines were approaching Ascom City from the southwest. On the west side of the Inch'on–Seoul Road D/5 established a perimeter atop Hill 186. Some 200yd beyond was a large knoll abutting the edge of Ascom, on which the company commander, 1stLt H.J. Smith, posted 2ndLt L.R. Smith's 2d Platoon. The main road passed through a cut on the knoll's southwest side with high ground on the other side. After dark an NK truck barreled down the road, was halted by 1st Platoon, Company A, 1st Tank Battalion, and its five occupants, one an officer, were taken prisoner. It was apparent the NK had no idea where the marine lines were. At 0545 hrs just as the sunrise brightened the sky, six T34 tanks of the 42d NK Tank Regiment approached the outpost from the east. Strung out for 200yd were an estimated 250 infantry on foot and riding on the slow-moving tanks. The infantry were from assorted units of the 18th NK Division in Seoul. They were ignorant of the marines' presence and they were eating and talking as the tanks rolled down the road. 2ndLt Howard reported the force to 1stLt Smith. Howard allowed the force to continue on toward Company D's position and both marine units opened fire with rifles, BARs, machine guns, 3.5in. "super bazookas," and 75mm recoilless rifles. The NK infantry were cut down in minutes. The attack was initiated by Cpl Okey

Douglas with a 2.36in. bazooka (1). He had slipped down the knoll and opened fire, knocking out the lead tank and damaging the second. The others continued down the road through a barrage of fire and were met by the marine tank platoon, which pumped 45 90mm rounds into the tanks and panicked infantry. In the end, 200 enemy dead and all six tanks were scattered on the road with only one marine lightly wounded. Marine battalion assault platoons were armed with the new 3.5in. M20 bazooka when they deployed*, but company and platoon headquarters were provided with the older 2.36in. M9A1 bazooka as a supplemental anti-tank weapon. Often condemned as ineffective against the T34, nonetheless the World War II weapon could knock one out from the side or rear. The "three-point-five," though, became the mainstay infantry anti-tank weapon and was widely issued to other UN and ROK forces. Weighing 14lb, the weapon was light for the capabilities it offered, and its HEAT rockets were 8.5lb. Its maximum effective range was 300 yards. The Soviet-made 32-ton T34 tank (2) had been perfected during World War II and proved deadly against German armor. The original model was armed with a 76.2mm gun, but those in Korea mounted an effective 85mm ZIS-S-53 (3). It also mounted a co-axial 7.62mm DTM machine gun and another in the bow (4) manned by a four-man crew. The accompanying NK infantrymen were armed with 7.62mm M1944 bolt-action carbines (with a folding bayonet) (5) and 7.62mm PPSh41 submachine guns (6).

*It is often assumed the 3.5in. bazooka was not developed until the 2.36in. was found inadequate against the T34, but the 3.5in. had already been standardized, although it had not been fielded to Army units in the Far East.

Army LVT(A)5 amphibious tanks of Company A, 56th Amphibious Tank and Tractor Battalion cross the Han River. They mounted a 75mm howitzer and three .30cal machine guns. The Marines' own 1st Armored Amphibian Tractor Battalion had been left in Japan – it was undermanned as many personnel had been sent to fill M26 tank crews. (USMC)

mortar barrages began to intensify and the marines prepared for a long night. They were deployed with 1 KMC northwest of Kimpo, RCT-5 south of Kimpo, RCT-1 southeast of Sosa, and the 32d Infantry south of Ascom in 1st MarDiv Reserve. The 17th Infantry would arrive on the 20th.

Regardless of the build-up, orders were issued in the late afternoon for RCT-5 to reconnoiter the Han the next day and cross it on the 20th. Once the enemy north of the Han had been defeated, the regiment would drive east to Seoul. Of the three ferry crossings, the one opposite Kimpo at Haengju was the best situated. Insufficient bridging materials were on hand to span the wide river, but there were large numbers of amtracs and Ducks, as well as two 50-ton pontoon rafts.

In preparation the 32d Infantry moved into the line left of RCT-1 at 1200hrs on September 19 relieving 1/1, and the marines side-slipped to the right. At the same time it was released back to 7th InfDiv control. Moving north, 1/1 relieved 1/5 on the south end of its line, while 2/1 KMC continued to advance in the north. The 1st Amphibian Tractor Battalion was relieved from supporting RCT-1 and marshaled at Kimpo, and the Duck company moved there too. The 1st Shore Party Battalion concentrated at Oeoso-ri. 1/5 Marines gained a position near Haengju, the crossing site. Little time remained for planning as the Reconnaissance Company would cross that very night and the main assault would commence at dawn. Units assigned the crossing included:

1st Marines
1st & 4th Battalions, 11th Marines
1st Amphibian Tractor Battalion
1st Engineer Battalion
1st Shore Party Battalion
2d Battalion, 1st KMC
1st Amphibian Truck Company
Reconnaissance Company, 1st MarDiv
Company A, 1st Tank Battalion
Company A, 56th Amphibian Tank & Tractor Battalion

At 2000hrs a 14-man reconnaissance company team swam across the Han, followed at 2100hrs by the rest of the company and engineers

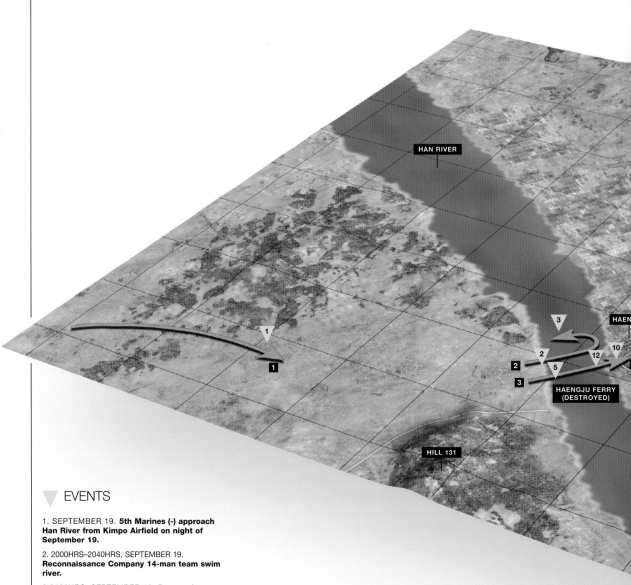

HAN RIVER

3

HAEN

2 12 10

2

5

3

HAENGJU FERRY
(DESTROYED)

1

1

HILL 131

▼ EVENTS

1. SEPTEMBER 19. **5th Marines (-) approach Han River from Kimpo Airfield on night of September 19.**

2. 2000HRS–2040HRS, SEPTEMBER 19. **Reconnaissance Company 14-man team swim river.**

3 2100HRS, SEPTEMBER 19. **Reconnaissance Company, reinforced by engineers, attempt to cross river aboard nine LVTs and are turned back by heavy fire from Hill 125.**

4. 0615HRS, SEPTEMBER 20. **15-minute artillery preparation by 1st & 4th Battalions, 11th Marines.**

5. 0630HRS–0650HRS, SEPTEMBER 20. **3d Battalion, 5th Marines cross river aboard LVTs in the order of Companies I, H, and G.**

6. SEPTEMBER 20. **I/3/5 Marines conduct two-pronged attack on Hill 125 (Objective 'ABLE') and secure it against heavy resistance.**

7. SEPTEMBER 20. **NK troops fleeing Hill 125 are attacked by four Marine Fighter Squadron 214 Corsairs.**

8. 0940HRS, SEPTEMBER 20. **G/3/5 Marines attack and secure Hill 51 (Objective 'BAKER').**

9. 0940HRS, SEPTEMBER 20. **H/3/5 Marines attack and secure Hill 95 (Objective 'CHARLIE').**

10. 1000HRS–1030HRS, SEPTEMBER 20. **2/5 Marines cross river, advance north to Hill 51, then move west to Objectives 'DOG' and 'ECHO' still aboard LVTs.**

11. SEPTEMBER 20. **2/5 Marines forced to dismount LVTs because of swamps outside Sojong.**

12. SEPTEMBER 20. **2/1 KMC cross river aboard LVTs and Ducks to protect 5th Marines' rear.**

13. SEPTEMBER 21. **1/5 Marines cross river, assemble near Hill 95, and prepare to lead next day's advance to Seoul.**

14. 1400HRS, SEPTEMBER 21. **5th Marines CP cross river and establish at Sojong.**

15. 1415HRS, SEPTEMBER 21. **D/2/5 Marines secure Objective 'ECHO.'**

16. 1415HRS, SEPTEMBER 21. **E/2/5 and F/2/5 Marines secure Objective 'DOG.'**

HAN RIVER CROSSING, SEPTEMBER 20, 1950

The 5th Marines' and the Korean Marines' commenced their assault crossing of the 400yd-wide Han River on September 20, while en route to Yongdungp'o. The attack on North Korean troops was supported by air strikes from Marine Corsairs in the surrounding area of Hill 125 (Objective 'ABLE').

Elms ⊠ 78 Indep.

Note: Gridlines are shown at intervals of 1 kilometer

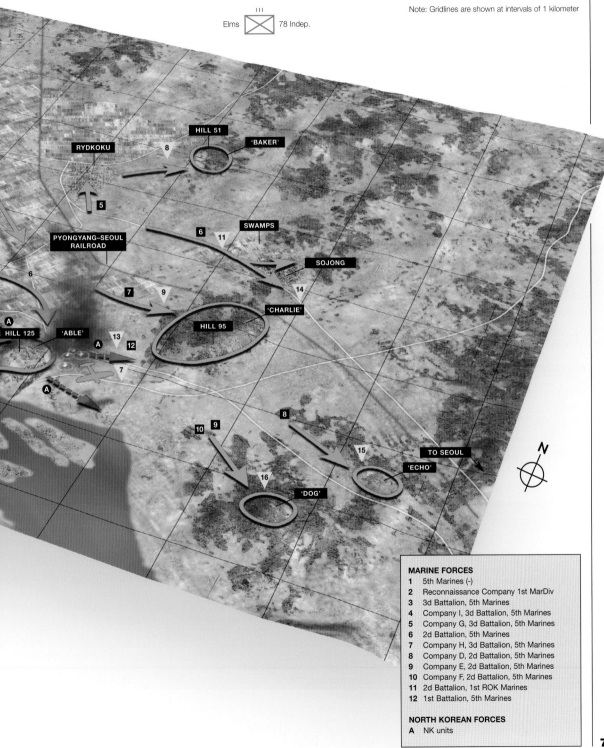

MARINE FORCES
1   5th Marines (-)
2   Reconnaissance Company 1st MarDiv
3   3d Battalion, 5th Marines
4   Company I, 3d Battalion, 5th Marines
5   Company G, 3d Battalion, 5th Marines
6   2d Battalion, 5th Marines
7   Company H, 3d Battalion, 5th Marines
8   Company D, 2d Battalion, 5th Marines
9   Company E, 2d Battalion, 5th Marines
10 Company F, 2d Battalion, 5th Marines
11 2d Battalion, 1st ROK Marines
12 1st Battalion, 5th Marines

NORTH KOREAN FORCES
A   NK units

aboard nine amtracs. The company was to seize and hold three hills, one on the river's edge and two others up to 2,000yd distance, until relieved by 3/5. It was too ambitious a mission for the small lightly armed unit. Finding no significant defenses, they signaled the amtracs to cross. When their engines turned over, the NK on Hill 125 overlooking the river opened fire. The amtracs attempted to cross regardless, but two were stranded in mud and abandoned when the order was given to withdraw. Casualties were light, but the undetected NK battalion on the hill had foiled the first crossing attempt.

Concerned with the image presented by marines unable to cross a 400-yd-wide water barrier, commanders relaunched the attack at 0630hrs after a short artillery preparation. Marines from 3/5 crossed under heavy fire, but no amtracs were lost and casualties were negligible. As Corsairs blasted Hill 125, I/5 overran it. The fleeing NKs were struck by the Corsairs. By 0940hrs G/5 and H/5 had secured Hill 51 north of 125 and Hill 95 northwest of 125. Soon after 2/5 crossed the Han and, still aboard amtracs, moved north to Hill 51 then west through Sojong to seize hills beyond Hill 95. Later, 2/1 KMC soon crossed to protect the rear of RCT-5, followed by 1/5 on the 21st. The Marines dug in for the night in a secure bridgehead north of the Han, suffering only 21 casualties.

Satisfied that *Chromite* was a success after so many dire predictions, Gen MacArthur enplaned after a final tour of the battlefield and returned to Tokyo on the 21st. That same day X Corps established its command post (CP) in Inch'on. RCT-7 arrived with 3/11 Marines, a much-needed artillery battalion. Fears of an NK attempt to retake Kimpo materialized as two enemy battalions were reported facing 3/1 KMC, but they made no serious attempt to cross the Han after suffering air attacks. Air support and artillery became more important as the lead marines were now beyond naval gunfire range. The 1st MarDiv was now split, with RCT-5 on the north side of the Han and the rest of the division to the south.

THE YONGDUNGP'O FIGHT

Yongdungp'o was an industrial town on the southwest side of the Han opposite Seoul. It was overlooked by high ground to its west. Between the hills and the town was the narrow Kalchon River, which presented only a minor obstacle. The east side of the Kalchon was backed by levees providing the NK defensive positions. The road and railroad bridges linking the two cities had been dropped. Separating Yongdungp'o from the Han was a 1½ by 2½-mile sandbar on which was situated the small Seoul airstrip. While Yongdungp'o could be reinforced and resupplied at night by ferry across the Han and the open sandbar, the town was isolated during daylight and the defense could not be sustained.

At dawn on the 19th RCT-1 advanced from Sosa to secure hills overlooking Yongdungp'o. Hills on the RCT's north flank adjacent to the Han were secured by 1/5, who then encountered mortar and small arms fire and a 500-man counterattack. This force was trapped on low ground and suffered 300 dead and 100 prisoners. Other groups of marshaling NK were pasted by artillery. 3/1 and 2/1 also met stiff resistance, and mines hindered the tank advance, but they secured objectives over-

Marines from the 1st Engineer Battalion assemble pontoon rafts into two 50-ton-capacity rafts to ferry tanks and vehicles across the Han River. Insufficient pontoons were available to span the 400yd-wide river. (USMC)

looking Yongdungp'o, inflicting 350 casualties on the North Koreans. Having relieved 1/5 adjacent to the river, 1/1 was hit by infantry and five T34s before dawn on the 20th. Daylight revealed 300 NK dead, two destroyed T34s and one captured. The marines suffered a setback as the powerful 4.5in. battery lacked the necessary fuses for its rockets, which did not arrive until the 28th. The fighting and maneuvering in the low hills adjacent to the river by 1/1 lasted through the 20th. In the south end of the RCT-1 zone, 2/1 repulsed an NK morning attack as it advanced on the highway toward Yongdungp'o and captured intact the bridge over the Kalchon River. To its south, the 32d Infantry was still moving up on line with the marines. NK hidden along the riverbank managed to ambush a wire-laying detail and some engineers, killing or capturing all of the men.

After a quiet night, (apart than the constant shelling of Yongdungp'o) 1/1 and 2/1 assaulted the town in the morning. The NK had concentrated their defenses in the north near the Han and in the southwest, but the central western portion was defenseless. In the north 1/1 seized the Kalchon bridge and fought through a series of fortifications to secure a foothold in the northwest corner of the town. The NK were deployed in sequential company strength lines on dikes and levees, but the American attack stalled because of confusion over requests for artillery support. This was because the artillery saw the 1/1 attack as heading north to Seoul, but because of the orientation of the NK positions, the battalion was attacking south. To the artillery, it appeared that their fire would hit the battalion rear. Once the misunderstanding was sorted out, however, marine fighters joined in blasting the enemy positions.

While most of the battalion was stalled, A/1 took an unexpected route across a mile of rice paddies and forded the Kalchon, concealed by high rice stalks. By noon they had penetrated well into the heart of Yongdungp'o without detection. The town's buildings were widely interspaced and they had good observation all around. Making their way almost all the way through the town, the company reported their position

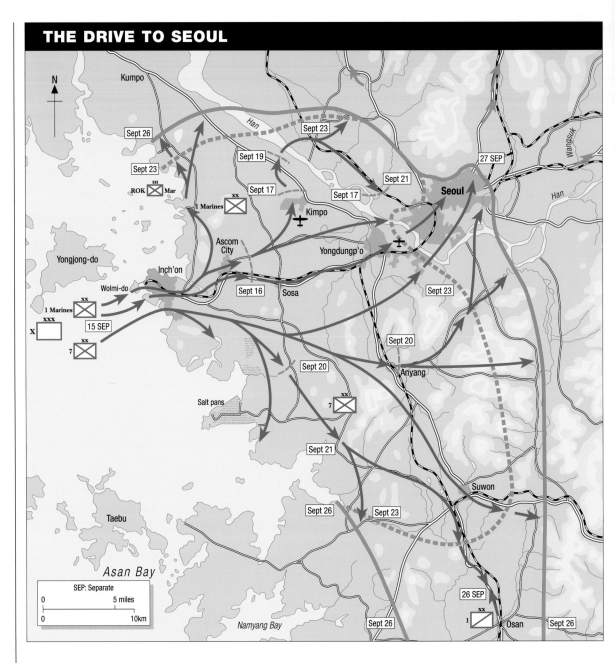

and the battalion commander ordered them to continue. They approached the junction with the Han River bridge highway and engaged surprised NKs, who scattered at the sight of marines deep inside the town. The marines took up an elongated defensive position atop a dike. From their vantage point they could see across the wide sandbar to Seoul and saw NKs withdrawing before a sister company's assault to the northwest. What appeared to be a coal pile was actually the main ammunition dump for the Yongdungp'o defenders, so it was blown up. A nearby building was found to be filled with US artillery, ammunition, equipment, and medical supplies, the last of great value to the now cut-off company – their radio had died. The NK made repeated attacks on the penetration. The Marines dug deep foxholes, which saved them at dusk when five unescorted T34s

A marine sniper fires at targets from the south side of the Han River. He is armed with a .30cal M1903A1 Springfield rifle fitted with an 8x Urertl telescope. The railroad bridge is the farthest to the left. (USA)

appeared. They ran the length of the dike five times, blasting the marines with 85mm and machine guns at 30 yards. Bazookas knocked out one and damaged two before they withdrew. One marine was injured. Before midnight five ground assaults were repulsed northwest. A captured NK officer managed to run off yelling warnings to his comrades to halt their attack as the marines were too strong. They heeded his advice. They left behind 250 dead and abandoned all the T34s.

In the south 2/1 crossed the bridge they had seized the day before, but were taken under heavy fire as they approached a second, this one crossing a Kalchon tributary. Casualties were high and the unit had suffered earlier losses. Striking from the northwest, 3/1 was committed to relieve the battalion and as they forded the Kalchon, met resistance on the levees. As night fell both battalions were dug-in on both sides of the Inch'on–Seoul Highway and remained outside the town. The 32d Infantry, facing little resistance, swung far to the south and cut the railroad and highway leading south to Suwon. They were positioned south of Yongdungp'o, but there was a 2-mile gap between them and RCT-1.

The loss of the ammunition dump to A/1 forced the enemy to give up Yongdungp'o and they left behind most of their heavy weapons. On the 22d RCT-1 cleared the town and took up position on the Han. They would cross into Seoul the next day.

ATTACKING THE MAIN LINE OF RESISTANCE

On the 21st RCT-5 was arrayed to approach Seoul along the railroad leading into the city from the northwest. On the 22nd 3/5 on the left flank seized Hill 216; 1/1 KMC took Hill 104 in the center overlooking the railroad; and 1/5 took Hill 68 between the railroad and the Han.

Two quality NK units had established a main line of resistance over 6,000yd long on higher hills behind the initial marine objectives. It stretched northeast from the Han across Hills 105-S, 56, 88, 296, and 338, a maze of hills and ridges cut by ravines, draws, and spurs with additional defenses dug into other hills to the rear. The 25th Rifle Brigade and 78th Independent Regiment were prepared to offer a stout resistance to defend Seoul. (There were three Hills 105 in the immediate area, one in each battalion zone, and were designated North, Central, and South to prevent confusion.)

Hill 216 on the north flank was taken with ease, but the Korean marines met much resistance on 104, although they eventually secured it. The marines of 1/5 experienced no difficulty taking 68 to the south. Problems began, though, when 3/5 continued from 216 to 296. They reported it secured, but three large southern spurs were still defended; Hill 296 was one of the NK centers of defense. Hills 56, 88, 105-N, 105-C, 72, and 105-S would all have to be cleared at great cost. On Hill 296 H/1 began to experience difficulties with company-size counterattacks and fire from the overlooking Hill 338. It took all three 1/5 companies to secure 105-S, finally achieving it late in the day, with 43 casualties. Having run into the center of resistance on Hill 56, 1/1 KMC was forced to withdraw to 104. Because of this, one 1/5 company was withdrawn to Hill 68 in order to support the Korean marines' renewed assault the following morning.

On the road to Seoul part of a marine squad digs in on a hillside for the night. A marine rifle squad had three .30cal Browning automatic rifles (BAR), while army squads had only one. In comparison, an NK section (squad) had one 7.62mm DPM light machine gun. (USMC)

The road to Seoul saw repeated ambushes and firefights. Every hill and ravine had to be cleared. Farther ahead are marine M26 tanks, followed by an M4A3 dozer-tank and a jeep. (USMC)

On the 23rd RCT-7 was finally ready for frontline operations. It had been doing mop-up to allow it a shakedown before commitment. The regimental CP and 3/7 crossed the Han and was positioned to the rear of RCT-5. The next day 2/7 northwest of Kimpo was relieved by the 187th ARCT, which had just arrived. The 7th would move to the northeast of RCT-5 to protect its flanks, rear and prevent the enemy from escaping north from the city.

On the morning of the 23rd 1/1 KMC attacked to straighten out the line. While preferring a flanking attack, the time remaining in the day forced 2/5, attacking through the KMC, to make a frontal attack on Hill 56, through which ran a railroad tunnel. No one realized that this was part of the main NK defense line. The hill was taken, but as D/5 continued on to the next ridge, named Smith's Ridge after the company

A Soviet-supplied T34/85 tank. This one appears to have been knocked out by aerial rockets and/or bombs. (USMC)

commander, they were hit heavy and losses were high. The survivors dug in for the night, but fortunately no counterattacks were received. The other two battalions held defensive positions through the day as 2/5 gained a foothold in the hills and they did fight off counterattacks. That same day, the 31st Infantry took over security of Suwon, 31 miles south of Seoul, and established a blocking position.

The attack on the 24th was again carried out by 1/5 to secure the remainder of Hill 56 and clear Smith's Ridge. F/5 had only 90 men, but D/1 was closer to full strength when it assaulted a large knob atop 56. It was soon pinned and there were constant grenade duels and efforts by both sides to outflank the other. Strength dwindled and the reserve company was committed to push on the assault. After a heavy bombardment, the 44 remaining effectives charged the knob, overrunning it, and then clearing much of Smith's Ridge. Only 26 effectives remained. The reserve, E/5, was sent to take 105-N, but an enemy strongpoint on 72 blocked their way and they were forced to wait a day. An estimated 1,500 dead NK were found on 56 and Smith's Ridge and another 1,750 on 296. The cost was high, but the marines had punched their way into Seoul.

At a staff meeting on the 23rd Almond proposed that RCT-5 continue its attack from the northwest, while RCT-1 be moved from Yongdungp'o and cross into Seoul from the southeast, with the goal of maneuvering the enemy out of the city. Smith opposed splitting his division and wanted RCT-1 and -5 to continue their attacks as planned and bring RCT-7 around to the north to flank the enemy, prevent his escape in that direction, and be in position to attack into the city center if the RCT-5 attack was halted by enemy resistance which was proving stronger than expected. The 32d Infantry, already to the south, could swing in from the southeast. Almond was pressing for Seoul to be liberated by September 25, three months to the day after the NK invasion. He was angered and on the verge of relieving Smith, but the political fallout would probably have ruined him[7].

At 0800hrs, after engineers had cleared the extensive mines, 2/1 crossed the Han at Sogang 3 miles west of the downed Han bridges aboard amtracs from Yongdungp'o. They linked up with C/5 in the afternoon. Because no pontoon rafts were available no tanks were able to accompany the battalion. Hill 79, 4,000yd from the crossing site, was the battalion's objective. The regimental CP and 1/1 came over next, with the battalion ordered to pass through the rapidly moving 1/2. Resistance was light and the railroad yard was seized at 1500hrs and the first American flag was raised in Seoul. That evening 3/1 crossed into Seoul, and the 1st MarDiv's regiments were all on the same side of the Han. A good deal of mopping up was required in the RCT-1 zone. The 32d Infantry continued its end run to the south and took up positions on the Han on the 24th where it was joined by the 17th ROK Infantry. The 32d Infantry was pushing south toward Suwon.

Far to the south, on the 23rd the NK forces fighting the Pusan breakout began to crumble. The battle for Inch'on was over, but Seoul had yet to be liberated.

---

[7] In 1944 marine LtGen "Howlin'Mad" Smith commanding V Amphibious Corps had relieved army MajGen Ralph Smith commanding 27th InfDiv on Saipan to create a serious rift between the two services, which eventually resulted in the marine Smith's reassignment.

AFTERMATH

THE BATTLE FOR SEOUL

By the 25th RCT-7 was on Seoul's north side, RCT-5 on the eastern hills overlooking the city, RCT-1 in the southeast suburbs, and the artillery positioned both northwest of Yongdungp'o and to the south. Marine amtracs brought the 32d Infantry across the Han 5,000 yards east of the main bridges. They occupied South Mountain (Nam-san) overlooking the city against little opposition. In the afternoon the 17th ROK Infantry was brought across, but received heavier artillery and mortar fire. With the 32d on the line the 17th would mop up. The 7th InfDiv was assigned a zone encompassing the southeastern third of the city.

The 1st MarDiv attack into Seoul commenced at 0700hrs on the 25th. As RCT-7 secured the north side and seized ground blocking the Seoul–Kaesong Highway, RCT-5, with 1/1 KMC and the reconnaissance company, punched in from the west, aiming for the city center. It first cleared the remainder of the hills. With 2/1 KMC, RCT-1, struck from the southwest, skirting South Mountain and driving toward the high ground on the city's northeast side. The Division reserve, 1st KMC Regiment (-) would take over as the city occupation force, while 3/187 ARCT provided rear area security.

The NK had established in-depth defenses throughout the city, fortifying the heavily constructed buildings and erecting hundreds of rice

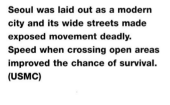

Seoul was laid out as a modern city and its wide streets made exposed movement deadly. Speed when crossing open areas improved the chance of survival. (USMC)

Barricades worked both ways. In many sectors the NKs constructed barricades from earth-filled rice bags and debris including vehicles at 200–300yd intervals. These marines, having gained a barricade, fire on sub-machine-gunners in upper floor windows. (USMC)

Marine infantrymen move toward Seoul with a platoon of M26 tanks interspaced in their column. This picture provides an example of typical terrain between Inch'on and Seoul, with rice paddies crisscrossed with roads and low hills. (USMC)

bag and debris barricades. AA fire was heavy over the city and several aircraft were downed.

After a morning of artillery preparation, 3/5 completed clearing Hill 296 and 2/5 assaulted 105-N, which was secured by 1545hrs; 1/5 then relieved 3/5. With the reconnaissance company, 1/1 KMC blocked the approaches to 216 and 296. RCT-5 had to make a 90-degree change in direction and moved toward Hill 105-S with tank support. This resulted in a gap between RCT-1 and -5. Hill 105-S, which was previously presumed secured, proved to harbor NK holdouts, which were routed. The two battalions fought their way 2,000 yards into Seoul in the vicinity of Hill 82. Meanwhile, as 2/7 to the north occupied its objective by noon on the road into the city, 1/7 patrolled the area between it and RCT-5. MajorGeneral Almond declared the city captured, a claim that was to prove premature.

An army M4A3 Sherman tank pushes damaged marine tanks into an LSU for evacuation to Japan and repair. The obsolete Sherman served on in the flamethrower and tank-dozer roles. (USN)

Shortly after 2000hrs on the night of the 25th, 1st MarDiv received unexpected orders to conduct an immediate night attack into the heart of Seoul. X Corps had reported that aerial observers detected NK troops withdrawing from the city. MajGen Smith questioned this report, believing they might be fleeing civilians. Enemy activity to the division's front gave no indication of a withdrawal. He sought confirmation from X Corps, and warned that a night attack into a strange city was dangerous. In his haste to declare the city secured, Almond ignored Smith's concerns and ordered him to carry out the attack immediately.

Artillery preparation commenced, and just as RCT-5 and -1 were about to depart at 0200hrs, a strong NK attack struck 3/1 with T34s and SU76s. This held up the assault and lasted until daylight. Seven NK combat vehicles were knocked out, 500 dead counted, and 80 prisoners were taken. As this fight was going on, an NK battalion attacked 2/32 on South Mountain. The line was restored with a loss of 400 NK dead and 175 prisoners captured.

On the 26th the attack continued, but RCT-7 to the north was also to be committed, reinforced by the Reconnaissance Company and the recently arrived 5/1 KMC. (There was no 4th battalion as Koreans considered "4" to be bad luck.)

The 7th would pinch out RCT-5 1,200yd beyond Government House and continued the advance beside RCT-7. Hilltop objectives were assigned on the northeast side of the city. The KMC was prepared to take over city security, but 3/1 KMC was attached to 3/187 ARCT for Kimpo Peninsula security. Ahead of the regiment D/7 advanced down the Inch'on–Seoul Highway and was ambushed, forcing it to withdraw.

On the 26th and 27th RCT-7 cleared the hills on the north side of Seoul. Elements of RCT-5 continued to clear the Hill 296 complex and other hills northwest of the city. It was up to RCT-1 to take the heart of the city. On the 26th 2/1 advanced on the streetcar line, while 1/1 cleared the railroad station beside South Mountain. Tanks had to blast the defended rice bag barricades that were erected every 200–300 yards. Snipers and submachine-gunners fired from windows and rooftops. By nightfall 2/1 had advanced 1,200 yards, while 3/32 attacked 3,000yd northeast overrunning a ridge on the east side of Seoul and cutting the highway. The 32d was reinforced by US 2/17, along with the 17th ROK Infantry. RCT-1 established contact with both RCT-7 and the 32d that day. On the 26th 7th InfDiv elements made contact with Eighth Army at Osan.

The 27th saw 3/7 clear the approaches to Hill 338 and 2/7 secured 343, but the former's attempt to take 342 failed, even though South Korean civilians had marked the NK minefield. In the meantime, 1/7 was engaged several miles to the west, resisting attacks by NK holdouts. As RCT-1 and -5 continued to fight their way into Seoul, 3/5 finished clearing Hill 296, while 1/5 took 338 overlooking the capitol, for which 3/5 was now heading. Then 2/1 took the French Consulate and the Middle School. In the early afternoon 3/5 reached the capitol, from which the NKs fled. Meanwhile 1/5 continued up the streetcar line and reached 338 by nightfall. Earlier 2/1 raised the US flag over the USSR Consulate.

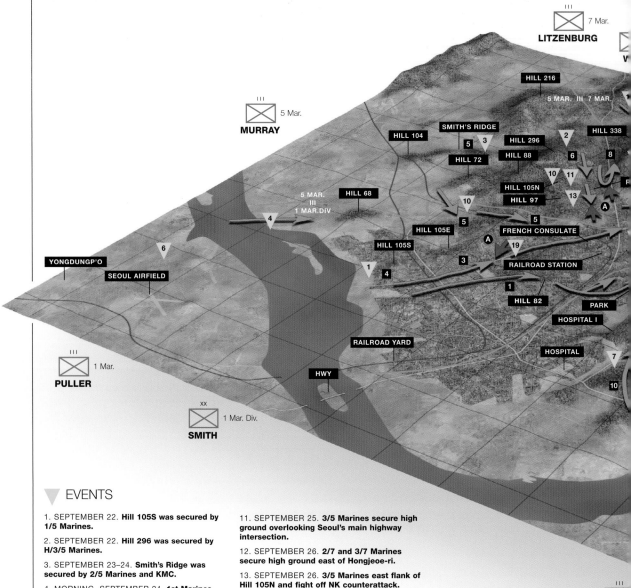

LITZENBURG   7 Mar.

HILL 216

5 MAR.   7 MAR.

MURRAY   5 Mar.

HILL 104   SMITH'S RIDGE
5   3   HILL 296   HILL 338
HILL 72   HILL 88   2
6   8
HILL 68   10   11
10   HILL 105N   13
HILL 97
HILL 105E   5   5
HILL 105S   FRENCH CONSULATE
5 MAR.   19
1 MAR.DIV   A   RAILROAD STATION
1   A   3
4   HILL 82   1
YONGDUNGP'O   PARK
SEOUL AIRFIELD   HOSPITAL I
6   HOSPITAL
RAILROAD YARD   7
PULLER   1 Mar.   10
HWY
SMITH   1 Mar. Div.

BEAUCHA

▼ EVENTS

1. SEPTEMBER 22. **Hill 105S was secured by 1/5 Marines.**

2. SEPTEMBER 22. **Hill 296 was secured by H/3/5 Marines.**

3. SEPTEMBER 23–24. **Smith's Ridge was secured by 2/5 Marines and KMC.**

4. MORNING, SEPTEMBER 24. **1st Marines cross Han River unopposed aboard 1st Amphibian Tractor and 56th Amphibious Tank and Tractor Battalions.**

5. AFTERNOON, SEPTEMBER 24. **32d Infantry cross Han River lightly opposed in morning aboard 1st Amphibian Tractor and 56th Amphibious Tank and Tractor Battalions followed by 17th ROK Infantry.**

6. SEPTEMBER 25. **1/11, 2/11, and 4/11 Marines positioned northwest of Yongdungp'o and 2/11 Marines and 96th Field Artillery Battalion inside the city provide fire support.**

7. SEPTEMBER 25. **32d Infantry secure South Mountain and southern side of Seoul.**

8. SEPTEMBER 25. **NK counterattack against 32d Infantry.**

9. SEPTEMBER 25. **3/1 and 1/1 Marines secure main road into Seoul and Hill 82, and fight off NK counterattack.**

10. SEPTEMBER 25. **2/5 Marine secure Hills 72 and 105N.**

11. SEPTEMBER 25. **3/5 Marines secure high ground overlooking Seoul's main highway intersection.**

12. SEPTEMBER 26. **2/7 and 3/7 Marines secure high ground east of Hongjeoe-ri.**

13. SEPTEMBER 26. **3/5 Marines east flank of Hill 105N and fight off NK counterattack.**

14. SEPTEMBER 26. **2/1 Marines advance into heart of Seoul.**

15. SEPTEMBER 26. **1/1 Marines secure west flank of South Mountain and link up with 32d Infantry.**

16. SEPTEMBER 26. **3/32 Infantry reaches east side of Seoul.**

17. SEPTEMBER 27. **D/2/7 Marines advance from Hongjeoe-ri, September 27 and are repulsed.**

18. SEPTEMBER 27. **2/1 Marines secure major highway intersection and high ground in east Seoul.**

19. SEPTEMBER 27. **3/5 Marines secure ROK Capitol.**

20. SEPTEMBER 27. **1/5 Marines secure Hill 338.**

THE BATTLE OF SEOUL, SEPTEMBER 25–27, 1950

The marine battle for Seoul began with the crossing of the Han River and the securing of various objectives surrounding the city limit. On September 26 marines penetrated the heart of the city, fighting amidst the dense modern infrastructure to secure the key objectives, including the ROK Capitol on September 27.

Note: Gridlines are shown at intervals of 1 kilometer

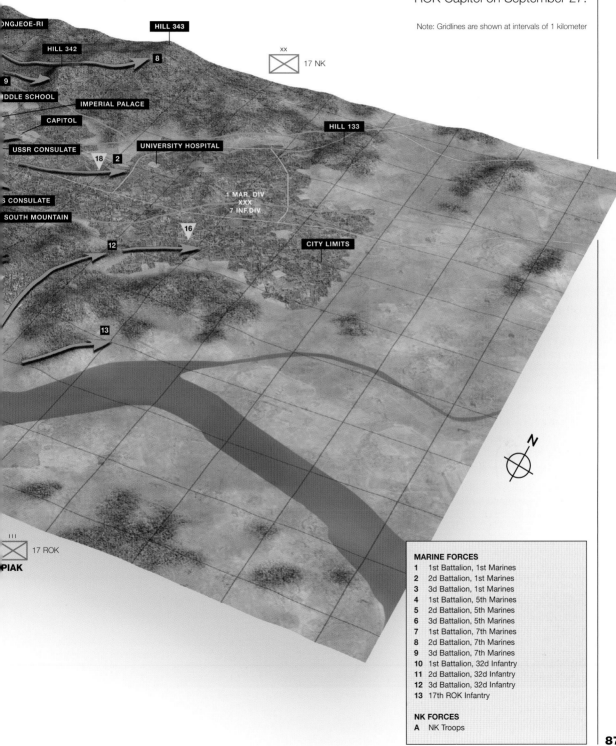

ONGJEOE-RI

HILL 343

HILL 342

8

9

XX
17 NK

IDDLE SCHOOL

IMPERIAL PALACE

CAPITOL

HILL 133

USSR CONSULATE

UNIVERSITY HOSPITAL

18 2

S CONSULATE

1 MAR. DIV
XXX
7 INF.DIV

SOUTH MOUNTAIN

16

12

CITY LIMITS

13

17 ROK

PIAK

MARINE FORCES
1 1st Battalion, 1st Marines
2 2d Battalion, 1st Marines
3 3d Battalion, 1st Marines
4 1st Battalion, 5th Marines
5 2d Battalion, 5th Marines
6 3d Battalion, 5th Marines
7 1st Battalion, 7th Marines
8 2d Battalion, 7th Marines
9 3d Battalion, 7th Marines
10 1st Battalion, 32d Infantry
11 2d Battalion, 32d Infantry
12 3d Battalion, 32d Infantry
13 17th ROK Infantry

NK FORCES
A NK Troops

A marine helicopter delivers a wounded marine to a floating dock inside Inch'on Harbor, to be carried immediately aboard the USS *Consolation* (AH-15). (USMC)

Defended barricades, snipers, and suicide attacks continued to plague the attackers. The 32d Infantry remained on South Mountain denying it to retreating NKs, but did clear some areas at its bottom. By evening RCT-1 had reached the east side of Seoul as NK resistance collapsed and they dug in for a comparatively quiet night.

Final operations inside Seoul were conducted on the 28th, with RCT-7 advancing up to 2,600yd while it cleared the high ground on the north side and its sector of the city. RCT-1 cleared the remainder of its zone, but encountered some resistance and many mines. The 1st MarDiv moved into barracks inside Seoul after displacing from Oeoso-ri. As mop-up continued by all units, preparations were made for the liberation ceremony. In the pre-dawn hours of the 29th the NK managed to launch counterattacks in both RCT-7 and 1 zones. In spite of holdouts and the danger of attacks, MacArthur and President Syngman Rhee arrived. Undeterred by gunfire and glass falling from the Government House dome, the two notables re-established the capital of the Republic of Korea and the republic's flag was hoisted at 1200hrs. Operations continued through the day to clear the city and its environs.

Redeployment and results

The pursuit of the fleeing NK forces began on the 28th, with the 1st Marines and the KMC clearing hills east of the city. The 7th Marines drove north toward Uijongbu, which they reached on October 3. As 3/5 pushed northwest, they reached Suyuhan on the 2nd. The 7th InfDiv established blocking positions to the east facing north and to the south. Other US and ROK units took up the pursuit, and the 1st MarDiv and KMC closed on Inch'on between October 5 and 7. A marine cemetery was established outside Inch'on as the division was informed they would mount out for another amphibious operation. This one would see them landing at the east coast port of Wonsan and would take them to the Chosin Reservoir.

The 1st MarDiv, barely able to field a regimental combat team, deployed a complete brigade to Korea, regenerated itself to full strength, deployed overseas with an aircraft wing, planned a complex amphibious operation, successfully executed the landing, fought its way inland, conducted three river crossings, cleared several urban areas, captured an important airfield, liberated the capital, and pursued the enemy out of the area, all in 64 days. The feat of the 7th InfDiv to rebuild to a full division and deploy in a few weeks was equally impressive.

The Inch'on landing and the following exploitation speeded the rapid disintegration of the North Korean forces at Pusan, completed the disruption of the NK supply line, denied reinforcements to the Pusan front, secured port facilities to support the offensive driving the NK north of the 38th Parallel, and achieved a political and psychological victory for the ROK and the UN. The 1st MarDiv was credited with taking 4,692 prisoners, inflicting 13,700 casualties, and knocking out 44 tanks. Their own losses were 415 dead, six missing, and 2,029 wounded. The 7th InfDiv killed some 4,000 NK and captured about 1,300, while losing 106 dead, 57 missing, and 409 wounded. Of the total casualties, 106 were Koreans (KATUSAs). KMC and ROKA casualties are unknown. Five marines won the Medal of Honor at Inch'on–Seoul.

After the Chinese entered the war on October 25 and pushed the UN forces south across the 38th Parallel, Seoul was again evacuated on January 4, 1951 and Inch'on on the 5th. On December 22nd LtGen Walker commanding Eighth Army ordered that Inch'on be totally destroyed, a defeatist order. Walker died the next day in a jeep accident and the order was fortunately not carried out; it would have required far too many resources to reconstruct the city when again liberated. Inch'on was not really occupied by the enemy this time as the US Navy presence neutralized its value. On March 15 Seoul was once again liberated, but this time by the ROK 1st Division, without ceremony.

DOG COMPANY PINNED DOWN, OUTSKIRTS OF SEOUL, SEPTEMBER 26 (pages 90–91)

On the morning of September 26, three US marine, the KMC, a US Army, and an ROK regiment closed in on Seoul from the northwest, west, southwest, and south. To spearhead the 7th Marines' advance, D/7 under Capt Richard R. Breen, was sent southwest on the Seoul–Kaesong Highway to secure the Sodaeman Prison on the northwest edge of the city. As D/7 approached Seoul between the steep slopes of Hill 296 on the right and Hill 338 on the left, they were greeted by cheering Koreans. The column was taken under fire from a water tower 400yd to the front and the civilians scattered (1). NKs then opened fire from the hillsides only 100yd away. The company deployed on both sides of the road returning fire, but was pinned down. The marines were unable to deploy flank security because of the civilian crowds. The company mortar section under 1stLt Paul P. Sartwell (2) set up two 60mm mortars (3) and immediately knocked out an enemy position. Totally exposed, the lieutenant directed the mortar fire and was hit three times before being put out of action. Two rifle platoons maneuvered to clear the slopes, but resistance was heavy. A tank-infantry relief force sent by the regiment was turned back. The company, faced with encirclement, all officers wounded, and casualties mounting, withdrew 1,000yd back up the road. The mortars delivered covering fire during the withdrawal. Carrying all of their dead and wounded, they established a perimeter on both sides of the road in the late afternoon. Before dark they received an airdrop of ammunition and supplies and prepared for a tough night. The NKs, though, contented themselves with remaining in their hill positions. The rest of the 2/7 was attacking eastward and the 3/7 also attacked east to secure a foothold on the north end of Hill 338. D/7 was relieved in the morning. Army and marine rifle companies were allocated an array of supporting weapons, but their distribution differed. A marine company had a machine-gun platoon of three sections, each with two squads armed with a Browning .30cal M1919A4 light machine gun. A section was generally allotted to each rifle platoon. Within the company headquarters was a mortar section with three 60mm M19 mortars. The marines concentrated 18 3.5-in. M20 bazookas in the battalion assault platoon, with two attached to each rifle platoon. Army rifle company weapons platoons had a mortar section with three 60mm mortars and a special weapons section with three 57mm M18 recoilless rifles (not used by the marines). Army rifle platoons had a weapons squad with a bazooka and an M1919A4 machine gun. The 60mm M19 mortar was the rifle company's workhorse, its resident "artillery." While artillery support was usually available, the benefit of the immediate fire that a company's own mortars could provide was invaluable. The M19 was essentially the same as the M2 used in World War II, but was provided with a selector lever on the tube's base plug allowing it to be drop-fired or trigger-fired. Some units deployed to Korea with the M2 and they were also issued to ROK units. Their ammunition was interchangeable with that of the Chinese 60mm Type 31. Ammunition included high explosive (4) and white phosphorous smoke (5) as well as illumination (parachute-suspended flares, not pictured). The maximum range was 1,985yd and its minimum was 50 yards.

THE BATTLEFIELD TODAY

nch'on and Seoul have grown immeasurably and are now large, modern cities virtually unrecognizable to veterans of the battles. This applies to most of the rural areas between the cities as well. Over a dozen bridges now span the Han River. The once undeveloped Yong-hong-do island offshore of Inch'on has been much expanded by landfill and now houses the Inch'on International Airport. Inch'on has a vast subway system connecting it to Seoul. The Inner and much of the Outer Tidal Basin have been backfilled and serve as industrial sites, while the causeway to Wolmi-do now serves as a bulkhead; much of the harbor enclosed by the causeway and Wolmi-do too have been backfilled. Wolmi-do is no longer recognizable as an island, though it still bears that name. The port has expanded and is now Korea's largest. Besides serving as a communications hub, Inch'on is also a popular tourist destination and is known for its wide variety of entertainment attractions, hotels, and restaurants. The Inch'on Peace Park hosts a 16ft marble statue of MacArthur gazing over the harbor, and small memorials are found on the three landing beaches. Other than these there is little to remind one of the war and the last large-scale amphibious operation in the history of warfare.

The American flag waves in front of Government House, September 29. The Republic of Korea flag has been hoisted on the taller pole to the right. Gunfire was still rattling when Gen MacArthur and President Syngman Rhee held a ceremony re-establishing Seoul as the capital of the ROK. (USMC)

BIBLIOGRAPHY

Alexander, Joseph H., *Battle of the Barricades: US Marines in the Recapture of Seoul*, Marine Corps Historical Center, Washington, DC (2000)

Appleman, Roy E., *South to the Naktong, North to the Yalu*, Office of the Chief of Military History, Washington, DC (1961)

Blair, Clay, *The Forgotten War: America in Korea 1950–1953,* Times Books, New York (1987)

Clark, Eugene F., *The Secrets of Inchon: The Untold Story of the Most Daring Covert Mission of the Korean War*, Berkley Publishing, New York (2003)

Field, James A., *History of United States Naval Operations: Korea*, Government Printing Office, Washington, DC (1962)

Hastings, Max, *The Korean War*, Simon & Schuster, New York, (1987)

Heinl, Robert D., Jr., *Victory at High Tide: The Inchon–Seoul Campaign*, J.B. Lippincott, Philadelphia (1968)

Langley, Michael, *Inchon Landing*, Crown, New York (1980)

Mantross, Lynn and Canzona, Nicholas A., *The Inchon–Seoul Operation, Vol. II, US Marine Operations in Korea*, Historical Branch, G-3, Headquarters, Marine Corps, Washington, DC (1955)

O'Ballance, Edgar, *Korea: 1950–1953*, Robert E. Krieger Publishing, Malabar, FL (1985)

Rottman, Gordon L., *Korean War Order of Battle: United States, United Nations, and Communist Ground, Naval, and Air Forces, 1950–1953*, Praeger Publishers, Westport, CT (2002)

Rice, Earle, *The Inchon Invasion*, Lucent Books, San Diego (1995)

Sheldon, Walt, *Hell or High Water: MacArthur's Landing at Inchon*, Ballantine Books, New York (1968)

Simmons, Edwin H., *Over the Seawall: US Marines at Inchon*, Marine Corps Historical Center, Washington, DC (2000)

Stanton, Shelby L., *America's Tenth Legion: X Corps in Korea, 1950*, Presidio Press, Novato, CA (1989)

Stanton, Shelby L., *US Army Uniforms of the Korean War*, Stackpole Books, Harrisburg, PA (1992)

Summers, Harry G. Jr., *Korean War Almanac*, Facts on File, New York (1990)

INDEX

Figures in **bold** refer to illustrations

38th Parallel 7, 8, 9, 11, 17, 23, 89

aircraft
    Chance Vought F4U Corsair 13, 57
      F4U-4B **14**, 57
      F4U-5N 57
    Convair OY-1 Sentinel 57
    Douglas R4C (C-47) **45**
    Grumman F7F Tigercat 57
    North Korean 53
    Sikorsky HO3S-1 **33**, 57
Almond, MajGen Edward "Ned" M. 25–26,
    27, 30, 31, **43**, 43, 45, 46, 47, 49
    Operation *Chromite* 55, 57, 81, 84, 85
amphibian tractors, Marine 34
    LVT(3)C **31**, 34
amphibious tank, LVT(A)5 **73**
amphibious truck, DUKW-353 ("Duck")
    2–ton **45**
Ascom City (Taejong-ni) 20, 23, 53, 63, 64,
    65
    tank ambush, Sept. 17: 64-65, **70–72**

Badoeng Strait, USS 57
Barr, MajGen David G. 27-28, 30, **43**, 45,
    46, 47
battlefield today 93
Beauchamp, Col Charles E. 28, **43**
Bradley, Gen Omar N. 47
Breen, Capt Richard R. **90-92**
British Infantry Brigade 11

Camp Pendleton 13, 14, 32
China/Chinese, Communist 7–8, 23, 29, 89
Chumunjin-up 44–45
Clark, Lt Eugene F. 51–52, 57
Collins, Gen J. Lawton 45, 47
commanders, American 24–28
commanders, North Korean 28–29
Communist invasion 8–9, 11, 22
Consolation, USS 88
Craig, BGen Edward A., USMC 13, 28, **43**
Curtis, Donald McB. 42

De Haven, USS **32**
Douglas, Cpl Okey **70–72**
Doyle, RearAdm James H. 30, 45, 46

East Channel (Tong Sudo) 19

Flying Fish Channel (So Sudo) 19, 48, 51,
    57

George Clymer, USS **15**

Haengju 20, 73
Han River **7**, 18, 20, 23, 48, 53, **79**, 81–82,
    83

crossing 69, **73**, 73, 76
    today 93
Harris, MajGen Field, USMC **27**, 28
Howard, 2ndLt **70–72**

Inch'on **50**, **77**
    battleground 17–21
    British Consulate Hill 17, 37, 61, **68**
    Cemetery Hill 17, 37, **50**, 50, 61, **68**
    evacuated 89
    fall of 9
    Harbor (Inch'on Hang) 18–19, 51
    Hill 94: 50
    Hill 117: 17, 50
    Hill 180: 63
    Hill 223: 63
    Hill 233: 50
    Inner Tidal Basin **17**, 19
    landings 44, 45–46, 47, 48–49, 50, **62**
      Beach Blue 49, 50, 55, 60, 62, 63
      Beach Green 49, 57
      Beach Red **32**, **44**, 49, **50**, 50, **54**,
      55, 60
      Beach Red, 1730–1850 hours **56**,
      61–64, **66–68**
    Observatory Hill 17, 37, 50, 61, 62
    Outer Tidal Basin **17**, 19, **35**
    Railroad Station **18**
    Sowolmi-do **17**, 18, 49, 60
    tidal changes 21
    today 93
    trenches **52**
    Wolmi-do (Moon Tip Island) **17**, 18, **37**,
    37, 46, 47, 48–49, 50–51, **52**
      causeway 61, 63, **64**, 93
      Operation *Chromite* 55, 57, 60, 61, 63
      Radio Hill 18, 57, 60
      seawall **56**, 61, **66–68**
      today 93
Inch'on-Seoul area **46**
Inch'on–Seoul Highway 19, 50, 63, 65,
    70–72, 79

Japan/Japanese 7, 10, 11, 12, 15, 25
Joint Chiefs of Staff 9, 12, 17, 45, 47
Joy, ViceAdm C. Turner 30, 45

Kalchon River 76, 77, 79
Kim Il Sung 29
Kimpo 53
Kimpo Airfield **14**, 20, 23, 37–38, 44, **45**,
    48, 49, 57, 65, 69
Kimpo Peninsula 17–18
Kobe, Japan 15, **16**, 54, 56, 57, 65
Korea 7
Korea, North (Democratic People's
Republic of Korea)
    established 7–8
    forces 36–38
Korea, South (Republic of Korea) 8

Korea Army, Republic of (South) 8, 9, 11,
    47
    Infantry Regiment (Separate), 17th
    (Seoul Regiment) **36**, 36, 55, 69, 83
      units 35–36
Korean Marine Corps (South Korea) 88
    Regiment, 1st (1 KMC) 14, 22, 35–36,
    63, 65, 69, 79, 80, 83, 84, 85
Korean People's Army (KPA) (North
Korea) 9, 12, **18**, 42, 47, 48, 52–53, 69
    "Air Force Division, 1st" 37–38, 65, 69
    and battle for Seoul 83–84, 85
    commanders 28–29
    established 8
    and Inch'on landing 60, 61, 64
    Independent Regiment, 78th 79
    infantry regiments 37
    Rifle Brigade, 25th 38, 41, 79
    rifle division 36
    Rifle Division, 9th 38
    Rifle Division. 18th 38, 41
    Rifle Division, 31st 38
    tank ambush at Ascom City **70–72**
    Tank Division, 105th 38
    units 36–38, 41
    Yi Homg-gwang Detachment 28–29
    Yongdungp'o fight **77**, 78
Korean Volunteer Army 28
Korean War, strategic situation **6**
Kunsan 44, 45, 49, 52

LCM (Landing Craft, Medium) **15**, 35, 54
LCVPs (Landing Crafts, Personnel and
Vehicles) 35, 49, **55**, **56**, 57, **66–68**
Lopez, 1stLt Baldomero 61, **66–68**
LST (Landing Ship, Tank) 21, **31**, **44**, **51**,
    54
LST-859 54
LSU (Landing Ship, Utility) 85

MacArthur, Gen Douglas 9, 11, 12, 17, **24**,
    30, 42–43, 45–46, 47, 76, 93
    biography 24–25
    landings 60, 65
    liberation of Seoul 88, **93**
Mansfield, USS 57
Mount McKinley, USS **48**, 57, 60

Naktong, battles of 13, 14, 22 *see also*
Pusan
National Defense Act 45
Nippon Flour Company **54**, 61

Operation *Bluehearts* 12, 43–44
Operation *Chromite* 17, 24 *see also*
battlefield today; plan, American
    command structure 30
    preliminaries and the approach 54–57
    assault: D-Day 57, 60
    Beach Red, 1730–1850 hours 61–64